W9-BNS-955

'One of the few publicly displayed representations of Lady Baillie herself is that in which she sits against a table, with her two daughters, Pauline and Susan, in the Thorpe Hall Room at Leeds Castle. It was painted by Etienne Drian (1885-1961).'

1927–1974

LADY BAILLIE AT LEEDS CASTLE

Alan Bignell

LEEDS CASTLE ENTERPRISES LTD.

FOREWORD

Leeds Castle was most famously described by the historian, Lord Conway, as the loveliest castle in the whole world, but it has also been called The Ladies' Castle because it was bestowed upon queens as the gift of kings. Although the last queen to hold it personally was Catherine de Valois, widow of Henry V, in the 15th century, it seems entirely appropriate that the last private owner should also have been a lady.

She was the Anglo–American heiress who, as Olive, Lady Baillie, made Leeds Castle her family home for almost half a century. Since her death in 1974, the castle has been in the care of the Leeds Castle Foundation and is, today, the second most popular tourist attraction in Kent, after Canterbury Cathedral.

Lady Baillie's highly successful determination to remain out of the public eye as much as possible has left very little written record of what life was like at the castle during her ownership. I have been very grateful for the help I have received from family members, friends and castle staff, past and present, who have shared personal memories with me and allowed me to use treasured photographs. Special thanks are due to former land agent John Money, historian and archivist David Cleggett, both of whom shared generously their memories and their research with me, and also to Leeds Castle Foundation land agent and curator Andrew Wells, whose editorial expertise has been invaluable.

Alan Bignell

CONTENTS

Chapter One

THE LADIES' CASTLE

As the clock in the tower of St Nicholas' Church in the village of Leeds, near Maidstone, chimed its farewell to 1899, three-quarters of a mile away Leeds Castle brooded over its reflection in the midnight dark water of its moat, indifferent to the arrival of the new century.

It had seen too many centuries come and go during the nine hundred years it had already survived, here in the heart of Kent, to be much moved by one more.

In its time it had been bestowed as the gift of kings upon beloved – and sometimes rather less beloved – consorts, provided political asylum and sanctuary from plagues, incarcerated prisoners and witnessed wonders of pomp and pageantry and sombre scenes of siege and sorrow.

It had been altered and added to, cherished and neglected, loved and unloved, and it had fuelled the frustrations of Englishmen and the envy of foreigners.

No, the nativity of the 20th century could hardly be expected to bring anything very new to this veteran, which had every reason to suppose it had seen it all.

The manor of Leeds could only dimly remember its Saxon origins, when it was given to Godwin, Earl of Kent, by Edward the Confessor. The castle's first stones were piled one upon another by a Norman baron during the 12th century reign of Henry I and it was acquired for the Crown during the reign of Edward I in 1281.

During the next three hundred years, the tradition of successive sovereigns giving it as a gift to their queens suggested it was a "ladies' castle". After that it again passed into private ownership, descending by inheritance through some of the great Kentish families, and by the dawn of the 20th century it belonged to the Wykeham Martins.

This family traced one descent from the 13th century

William, Lord Leyburn whose daughter, Juliana, became known as the Infanta of Kent because of her enormous wealth and landowning influence. It was Leyburn who sold Leeds Castle to Edward I, who gave it to his Queen Eleanor and so began the "ladies' castle" tradition.

Leeds Castle came into the Wykeham Martin family when its previous owner, General Philip Martin, died in 1821 and left it to his kinsman Fiennes Wykeham, together with £30,000 to be spent on repairing and improving the building. Wykeham added Martin to his own name.

The new owner and his family had taken up residence amid appropriately demonstrative celebrations by a staff for whom the new arrivals promised continuing employment and they set about spending the general's bequest on essential building work, suitable furnishings and works of art of various kinds.

There was plenty of work that needed to be done. The castle mill and the barbican were in ruins and the gatehouse had to be completely rebuilt. A tower at the side of the courtyard was on the point of collapse, the main building was not a lot better and much of the gloriette was a ruin, part having fallen into the moat a century before.

In short, the castle which traced its origins back to post-Conquest Kent, and parts of which had already been rebuilt a number of times since then, was showing its age and needed to be practically rebuilt again.

Fiennes decided the rebuilding this time should be in the Tudor style and by February 1822 his architect, William Baskett, had completed plans for a new castle.

Before the work began, the family took the unprecedented step of opening the castle to the public for two days, Friday and Saturday, 8 and 9 March, 1822. The opportunity to view the property was taken by what the local paper called "vast numbers" of visitors who tramped through the house and grounds, admiring the furniture and hangings and also the repairs that had already been carried out by the new owner.

That work, incidentally, had uncovered a skeleton close by a water jug, evidence of some long-ago bricking-up about which recorded history seems to have nothing to tell us.

The public open days over, parts of the old buildings were completely demolished and in May that year the first stones of the two entrance towers to the new castle were laid. By July, part of the roof was on and in mid-September, to the accompaniment of pealing church bells, band music and general rejoicing, Fiennes' son Charles celebrated his 21st birthday by seeing the final raising of the roof and the completion of the first stage of the old castle's latest reincarnation.

In 1822, the Rochester-born lawyer, antiquarian and architectural artist William Twopeny drew a number of views of the castle, and took a great and not always welcomed interest in the work while it was in progress. In fact, the main staircase, of polished oak, since replaced by the present stone stairway, was designed by him.

Now began the work of preserving the gloriette, which went on throughout much of 1823. The bridge connecting the central and the north islands, which had been two-storeyed with a pitched and tiled roof, was rebuilt in stone and castellated. A small cupola that had topped the tower at the gloriette end of the bridge was removed, the tower itself was heightened and a number of other more minor alterations were also made at this time. The work of recreating the gardens and grounds went on until 1835. The entrance into the park from the crossroads where the Leeds and Hollingbourne roads crossed the Maidstone-Folkestone road was moved to its present position and the moat, which had become choked with weed, was cleaned out.

During the course of the work, a good deal was thrown away and in a footnote to his chapter on the *Recovery of Manuscripts* in *Curiosities of Literature, Vol. I* (published in 1866), Isaac Disraeli, father of the one-time Maidstone MP and later Prime Minister, Benjamin Disraeli, wrote: "One of the most curious modern discoveries was that of the Fairfax Papers and correspondence by the late J N Hughes of Winchester, who purchased at a sale at Leeds Castle, Kent, a box apparently filled with old coloured paving tiles; on removing the upper layers he found a large mass of manuscripts of the times of the Civil Wars, evidently thus packed for concealment; they have since been published and add most valuable information to this interesting period of English history."

Apparently, some of the papers were cut up and others were used by Maidstone milliners for thread-papers but the rest were rescued by a Maidstone banker, John Newington Hughes, who sold them to a publisher. They were subsequently published in four volumes of Fairfax correspondence.

The work of restoring the castle cost a great deal of money, several thousand pounds more than was covered by the General's bequest, but it put Leeds Castle firmly on the map of properties to be visited. When Victoria, Duchess of Kent (mother of the future Queen Victoria) travelled through the county from Dover on her way to Sussex, in August 1825, she expressed a wish that the Castle gates should be open so that her carriage could drive through, allowing her to see the new castle, although she did not wish to stop to be greeted by the family because she would be in too great a hurry.

The refurbishment also plunged the family into financial difficulties, so that by 1830 their debts amounted to well over £9,000 – a very considerable sum, equivalent to more than £1.5million in today's terms. Fiennes was advised that, if he was to avoid imprisonment, he had to sell the castle contents and live abroad, leaving the castle in the hands of trustees.

In the meantime, Fiennes' son Charles, by now 29 years old, married Lady Jemima Mann, daughter of Earl Cornwallis of Linton Park, south of Maidstone, in April 1828. Although parental consent to the marriage was won only with an undertaking that none of his bride's money would be spent on restoring the Wykeham Martin family fortunes, it did mean that Charles was able to spend more of his own money than would otherwise have been possible.

So, when the sale of the castle contents took place in April 1830, Charles was able to buy some of them himself. Family portraits and other items were excluded from the sale and remained together, some of them being bequeathed to the Leeds Castle Foundation in 1984 by Mr Fiennes Wykeham Martin, whose father had sold the castle to Mrs Wilson Filmer (later Lady Baillie) in 1926.

After his marriage, Charles lived at Egerton House near Ashford and Leeds Castle was unoccupied for the next fifteen years. Although Fiennes visited it from time to time during this period, it was not until towards the end of his life that he came back to live in almost reclusive and relatively impoverished retirement in poorly furnished rooms in the castle, where he died in September 1840.

Charles Wykeham Martin inherited both Leeds Castle and other family property on the Isle of Wight, where he was Liberal MP for Newport in 1841-52 and again in 1865-70. Between those two periods, he was Liberal MP for West Kent in 1857-59. His wife, Jemima, died in 1836 and he married again. His second wife, Matilda, was a cousin of the novelist Anthony Trollope and together they laid the foundations for the restoration of the family fortunes.

Charles loved Leeds Castle but the neglect that had resulted from his father's financial difficulties meant that even more work now needed to be done on parts of the building. It was some time before Charles was able to afford to embark on the new work but once started he spent the rest of his life restoring the castle.

Before he died, aged 69, in September 1870, he had made the restoration of the gloriette his "main amusement", having published in 1869 *The History and Description of Leeds Castle, Kent.*

After Charles, the castle descended through the family to Fairfax Wykeham Martin (1887-1952), who became the last member of the family to own it.

It was during the Wykeham Martin family ownership that several rather odd legends seem to have been introduced to the castle. One claimed that if a hawk were brought into it, the death of the owner would occur. Another hinted at a haunting by the ghost of Joan of Navarre and there was also said to be a small dog that appeared and disappeared in some of the rooms.

One story related by Alice Pollock in her *Portrait of My Victorian Youth* (1971) tells how her great-uncle was lying, half asleep, on the wide window-sill in the room known as Henry VIII's room, upstairs in the old castle when a sudden feeling of fear impelled him to get up hurriedly and move back into the room. He had only just stepped away from the window-sill when the whole window-frame and seat fell into the moat below. The story concluded: "If he had remained sitting there, he would have been drowned."

During the turn of the century boom in picture postcards, Leeds Castle was a popular subject and in 1913 Lord Conway (1856-1937), art critic and explorer, was moved to make his often-quoted comment that this was the loveliest castle in the world.

Fairfax Wykeham Martin never lived at the castle. His home was a farm near Canterbury. When he offered the castle for letting in 1925 it was described by the agents as being substantially built of stone, with an Entrance Hall, Great Hall, Staircase Hall with wide oak staircase, WC and Cloakroom, large and smaller Drawing Rooms, Library, Dining Room, Banqueting Hall and small smoking room. There were also an original chapel, kitchen, scullery, housekeeper's rooms, servants' hall and stoke-hole for the heating.

On the upper floors there were "about twenty" principal bed and dressing rooms, maids' workroom, housemaids' pantries, hot linen cupboard, WCs and fourteen servants' bedrooms.

Features included Jacobean oak panelling, carved stone Tudor chimney pieces and fireplaces, original firebacks and a carved oak overmantel.

Water was supplied from a spring in the park and there were grass walks around the moat featuring formal flower borders, as well as a kitchen garden and glasshouses. There was stabling for horses, garaging for six cars, shooting over the 3,200 acre estate and fishing in the moat and several ponds on the estate.

All this for £1,000 a year, plus five percent on the outlay for improvements. This, then, was the castle that Mrs Arthur Wilson Filmer found when, after Fairfax Wykeham Martin had changed his mind and decided that instead of letting the castle, he would sell it (though only to a family with Kentish connections, he stipulated), she came to see if it promised to fulfil her ambition to own a property that she could make into a delightful and unique country home for herself and her family.

Chapter Two

WHO WAS LADY BAILLIE ?

The Mrs Wilson Filmer who came to view Leeds Castle in 1926 was the twenty-six year-old wife of Arthur Thomas Filmer Wilson Filmer.

She was born in 1899 in the USA, Olive Cecilia Paget, elder daughter of Almeric Paget, later to become first (and last) Baron Queenborough and his American first wife Pauline, who was the daughter and heiress of the Hon William C Whitney.

Olive's grandfather, William Whitney, was the US Navy Secretary in President Grover Cleveland's first administration (Democrat, 1885-89). He died in 1904 leaving a substantial fortune founded on the New York tramways system. Her paternal great-grandfather was Field Marshal the Marquess of Anglesey, KG, who commanded the cavalry at the Battle of Waterloo. On her father's side, the Paget family ancestry included William, first Lord Paget KG, who was one of Henry VIII's principal Secretaries of State.

She had a sister, Dorothy Wyndham Paget, who was born in 1905 and who, having founded a hospital for Russian émigré officers in Paris, went on to become very much more famous as a successful race-horse owner. Her blue and yellow racing colours flashed first past the post at the 1934 Grand National and at a number of classic races, including the 1943 Derby.

Their mother died in 1916 and the two sisters inherited a very considerable fortune. They had an uncle who was married to the sculptress Gertrude Vanderbilt, who thus became Gertrude Vanderbilt Whitney. It was she who designed the Titanic memorial in Washington, USA and she also designed, at the request of Lord Queenborough, the elaborate monument that distinguishes Pauline Paget's grave in the churchyard at Hertingfordbury, Hertfordshire, where Lord Queenborough, who died in 1949 and Dorothy Paget, who died in 1960, are also buried.

Olive spent part of her youth in France, where she was

educated, and in 1918 she served briefly as a war-time nurse.

Her first marriage, in 1919, was to the Hon Charles John Frederick Winn (1896-1968), the second son of Lord St Oswald and a serving officer with the 10th Hussars. The St Oswald family home was at Nostell Priory in Yorkshire.

The wedding was at St Margaret's Church, Westminster, and *The Times* recorded that the bride, who was given away by her father, Lord Queenborough, wore a white Windsor satin gown veiled in old family Brussels lace, which also formed the Court train. In her hair, securing her tulle veil, she wore a silver ribbon and orange blossom, and more orange blossom at her waist. She carried a bouquet of white lilies.

Her attendants included two small trainbearers, one boy, one girl, who were followed by two more children, again a boy and a girl, and four older bridesmaids, one of whom was her sister Dorothy.

The best man was fellow officer Viscount Ednam, and a guard of honour, provided by the bridegroom's regiment, formed an arch of swords over the couple.

The newly-weds moved into a house in Hill Street, London where their daughters, Pauline and Susan, were born in 1920 and 1923. Between 1919 and 1926, Olive rented at least nine different houses in the UK and abroad, but it was while the family were living at Hill Street that the house was comprehensively burgled and it was the need to replace the stolen furniture and other items that introduced Olive to what became a lifelong enthusiasm for collecting beautiful things.

The marriage lasted six years, ending in divorce in 1925, and was followed by a second one, this time to Arthur Wilson Filmer. The newly-weds rented Bawdsey Manor in Suffolk, and while they were there, Olive's pet monkey was accused of causing damage to carpets to an extent estimated in court at £2,000.

It was this marriage that brought Olive to Kent. Her new husband, an enthusiastic big game hunter and collector of tapestries, fine fabrics and old English furniture, was maternally a member of the Filmer family of East Sutton Park near Maidstone, which he had inherited in 1916. He later inherited his father's estate near Beverley in North Yorkshire and bought nearby Rowley Hall in 1938, where he bred cattle. He shared his wife's enthusiasm for – almost fascination with – the cinema and films and it was he who was responsible for her first sight of Leeds Castle, which began her lifelong love affair with "*the loveliest castle in the world*".

The Wilson Filmers were not the only ones who contemplated the castle as a possible English home. Owning an English castle has always been a status symbol and in the 1920s the world's great status seekers were the Americans. In 1903, William Waldorf Astor had bought the 14th century Hever Castle and lavished a large fortune on its restoration and in 1925 the American publishing millionaire, William Randolph Hearst, had set his heart on owning an English castle, too. He cast an acquisitive eye in the direction of Leeds, in Kent, and had the managing director of his English company look the place over for him. When she reported that in her judgment it would cost about £4,000 to make part of it fit to live in, Hearst decided to pass it over in favour of St Donat's Castle in Glamorganshire.

So the field was left clear for the Wilson Filmers. Olive had already fallen in love with the castle, despite the general air of neglect that clung to it. It was now more than a century since its last major overhaul by Fiennes Wykeham Martin and it had not been lived in since 1924. Parts of the grounds were overgrown, though not the green on which Leeds village cricket club played (later to become known as the Cedar Lawn). But the Wilson Filmers were able to afford to rescue it from the threat of dereliction and in 1926 it was bought (although it took until 1927 for the paperwork to be completed) for £180,000, with the expectation that about £100,000 would need to be spent on restoring it.

The marriage did not long survive the purchase. The couple parted company very soon after the property became theirs and in November 1931 the Lady of Leeds Castle married for the third and last time. Arthur Wilson Filmer died in 1968.

Olive's third husband was Sir Adrian William Maxwell Baillie, fifth baronet, of Polkemmet in Scotland and it is as the Hon Olive, Lady Baillie, that her place has become established in the castle's history as its longest individual owner.

Sir Adrian was born in 1898, educated at Eton and at The Royal Military College, Sandhurst and succeeded to the title when he was sixteen, after his brother was killed in action in 1914. He served as a lieutenant in the Scots Greys in France in 1918 and later joined the Diplomatic Service, acting as a second secretary in Washington from 1924 to 1928.

In 1931, aged thirty-three, Sir Adrian was a wealthy, good-looking, easy-going man, whose first attempt to become Conservative MP for Linlithgow in the May 1929 election had been frustrated when his Labour opponent, Glaswegian Emmanuel Shinwell, took the seat with a 6,822 majority.

But then the Wall Street crash imprinted its indelible scar on 1929 and throughout 1930 unemployment clawed its way up towards the three million level. Linlithgow was a Scottish mining constituency where there was a great deal of unemployment. The shale mines had closed and the miners blamed the Labour government's Coal Mines Act for the fact that they were now working ninety hours a fortnight instead of eighty-eight and earning 4d less for each shift they worked.

In August, 1931 a coalition National Government was formed under the Labour Prime Minister, Ramsay MacDonald, but the country was close to bankruptcy. The situation was so serious that King George V took a £50,000 a year pay cut for the duration of the crisis. When the General Election was called for 28 October, Sir Adrian Baillie was among the candidates who shared the landslide Conservative victory. He took the Linlithgow constituency for the Unionists, unseating Emmanuel Shinwell.

The election gave the Conservatives a majority of almost 500 seats in the new National Government that was formed under Ramsay MacDonald, in which Labour held only fifty-two seats.

The election victory won, the marriage of Sir Adrian Baillie, MP and the Hon Olive, Mrs Wilson Filmer took place on 4 November, 1931 at Holy Trinity, Brompton. *The Times* reported that the bride was given away by her father, Lord Queenborough, and that she wore a long coat of royal blue cloth trimmed down one side of the front with black fox fur. The high collar of the coat was of the same fur. She wore a hat of matching blue felt trimmed with a black osprey at one side and she had a large spray of pink and white orchids pinned to her coat.

The reception was held at the Balfour Place home of the bride's sister, the Hon Dorothy Paget, and the bridal couple afterwards spent a honeymoon in Paris.

Lady Baillie was described, in her mid-thirties, as a good-looking but forbidding woman with a certain charm and an indefinable air of authority. She was of about average height, slim, elegant, with very direct (some said piercing) blue eyes. She had a great deal of energy that expressed itself in drive and initiative rather than physical activity. She could be intimidating in her assumption that she would get her own way.

She could also be autocratic – "schoolmistressy" was one description that was used of her – and she treated all who worked for her with an almost feudal maternalism. In that she was not exceptional because many employers still had that sort of relationship with their workers. Although she was strong-willed, she could also be very gentle, with an endearing capacity for making her guests feel at home.

A family friend, the celebrated debutante and socialite Miss Margaret Whigham, who later married the Duke of Argyll and excited newspaper editors and their readers from 1959 until 1963 with a series of court cases leading to one of the most sensational divorce cases of the century, described Sir Adrian as good-looking and charming, but "somewhat overshadowed by his undoubtedly domineering wife".

In her autobiography, *Forget Not* (W H Allen, 1975), the duchess admitted that, before her first visit to Leeds Castle in 1936, when she was Mrs Charles Sweeny, she was warned that Olive was an eccentric woman and so shy that she could take two or three days before meeting a new guest in her house. Sometimes, she was not seen by her guests during a whole weekend.

Afterwards, the Duchess wrote: "I am sure many momentous decisions were made at Leeds, when Olive was closeted in her room, having mysterious meetings with Very Important People. But although an undoubted power in the political world she was scarcely known to the public at large. She had written to all the newspaper owners informing them that she disliked publicity and wished never to be mentioned in the press. And she rarely was."

Other contemporaries have questioned whether "shy" was quite the right word although all agree that Lady Baillie was, certainly, reserved; a woman who "kept herself to herself" and who protected the privacy of others, too. She had a large circle of acquaintances but a relatively small number of close friends. She bestowed trust cautiously, but once given it was not readily withdrawn and she was regarded as a good friend in need. That constancy applied equally to her staff who, once she had accepted them, could rely on her to look after them well and faithfully. Any that became ill were taken to London doctors and specialist clinics if that became necessary.

She was unobtrusive; in company she preferred to listen while others talked, but she could keep a conversation going if it looked like flagging at all and she gave the impression of always being in control of whatever situation in which she found herself. She was inclined to be dismissive of censure of any kind, tended to write her own rules and live by them and surrounded herself with influential friends who could – and did – smooth many of life's difficulties. What she lacked in natural spontaneity, she made up for in meticulous attention to detail.

One of her great friends was the Austrian singer, Richard Tauber. His wife, Diana, in her book *My Heart and I*, wrote of Lady Baillie's sudden smile and whimsical humour.

Almost certainly, she did not, in fact, wield any political power, or even wished to, but the hospitality for which Leeds Castle became famous undoubtedly brought together people who did wield such power and whose friendship and confidences she enjoyed.

The Baillies had one son, Gawaine, born in 1934 and christened in the church at Leeds. Sir Adrian went on to become Conservative MP for the Tonbridge division of Kent in March 1937, a seat he occupied until he retired in June 1945. He and Lady Baillie were divorced in 1944, and he died of pneumonia in London in January 1947.

Like her sister, Dorothy Paget, Olive certainly shunned personal publicity but she was far from reclusive, and she earned a reputation as a gracious hostess. However, when journalists began to want to chronicle some of the activities of this star of the social scene, she put her foot down very firmly. Leeds Castle was her country retreat and she used whatever influence she had to see that it remained just that. Very little indeed was published about life at the castle throughout her occupancy.

Her education and upbringing in France had equipped her to speak fluent conversational French, which gave her a firm grasp of all the implications of the suggestions made to her by the French advisers and suppliers with whom she dealt. When she spoke, it was in a firm, almost a deep voice and the walnut cigarette holder through which she smoked aromatic Turkish cigarettes was so constant a part of her ensemble as to be almost a distinguishing feature.

These were days before the dangers of tobacco smoking were understood in the way they are today, but in other ways she was very health conscious, avoiding all contact with anyone who had even a mild cold, including family members. Her daughters sometimes had to carry on a conversation with her from one end of a long room to the other to minimise the risk of passing on whatever germs they were suspected of harbouring at the time.

She was a devotee of the cinema, with which, of course, she grew up, and she was known, on occasions, to watch films in the Saloon while guests amused themselves in other parts of the same room. Her love of flowers was evident in the luxurious arrangements that were an important part of the decor of the castle interior. She preferred horse riding and croquet to the more energetic pastimes like golf and tennis and she enjoyed gambling, although later in life she favoured bridge and canasta. She did not care for shooting, but she tolerated it as an inevitable part of life on a country estate.

Lady Baillie loved dogs, too, and owned many during her lifetime. When they died, they were buried beside the Cedar Pond in the castle grounds, each grave marked with its own headstone, three of which remain.

She was very conservative indeed about food, always preferring simple, plain cooking to more exotic dishes, even though her guests were offered much more lavish menus. At table she drank only water with her meals.

Although she rode about the park and estate, usually side-saddle, and enjoyed strolling in the castle gardens, she was not a passionate "outdoor woman". She loved children and the daughter of one of the gardeners, many years later, treasured the memory of the "very nice lady" who helped her dig her own little garden plot at Wier Cottage.

Most of her staff, men and women alike, regarded her with genuine respect and liking and she continued to be remembered, twenty-five years after her death, almost unanimously as "a lovely lady" with a compassionate and practical concern for the welfare of those she employed and their families.

She was exceptionally well-organised, having a daily diary typed out for her, detailing the comings and goings of guests and accompanying staff so that she always knew when they arrived, what they ate, and when they left. She expected to be kept informed of even the most petty of cash expenditures, down to the 2d spent on buying an evening newspaper.

When she travelled, the suitcases that went with her contained lists of contents and she kept a constantly up-dated inventory of everything she owned. She became a keen, almost a compulsive and sometimes an impetuous buyer of antiques and art works of all kinds, but it was not the age of her purchases nor their value that enticed her so much as their appeal to her own taste. She was a collector, but not a hoarder, happily parting with some laboriously acquired objects in order to acquire others.

She was said to have very little sense of history, being far more concerned with the "here and now" and she regarded her life as her own business and no-one else's. As a result, we have more detailed records of some of the people who lived at Leeds four and five hundred years ago than we have of the occupancy of the last lady of the Ladies' Castle.

During the last years of her life, a respiratory illness, probably caused and certainly aggravated by her smoking habit (when she stopped smoking, on the advice of her doctor, it was already too late), made it necessary for her to resort to a wheelchair and after she died, in 1974, at her London home, it was Leeds Castle that became her lasting memorial. At her own request, she was cremated and her ashes scattered. Instead of bequeathing the castle to any one person, it was left to the care of a charitable trust as a national rather than a dynastic heirloom of the kind with which it was historically familiar. The sheer scale of Leeds and the cost of maintaining and running the castle and park, together with the high level of estate duty payable on her death, meant that the decision to bequeath it to a charitable trust became almost inevitable.

After her death, on Monday, 9 September, 1974, at the age of 75, *The Times* carried an obituary notice in which "a correspondent" wrote: "Apart from the love of her children and the care of her staff, the embellishment of Leeds Castle became her life work. She will be remembered by her friends as a woman of rare distinction, of immensely strong character, with the warmest human feelings for people, entirely irrespective of their worldly position."

There is no doubt that she was a woman of strong character, used to having her own way, who could temper her authority with charm but also enforce it with firmness and who was capable of commanding great loyalty and sincere affection from people who knew her.

But the lingering element of mystery with which her reserve and avoidance of any kind of publicity has surrounded the almost half-century of her ownership will, inevitably, haunt the castle for as long as it stands, adding its own characteristic epoch to the long history of one of Kent's — indeed, England's — most treasured gems.

The descendants of Lady Baillie

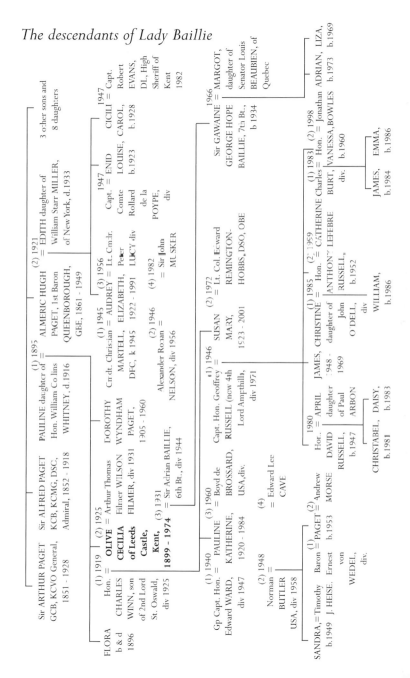

Sir ARTHUR PAGET
GCB, KCVO General,
1851 - 1928

Sir ALFRED PAGET
KCB, KCMG, DSC,
Admiral, 1852 - 1918

PAULINE daughter of (1) 1895 = ALMERIC HUGH
Hon. William Collins
WHITNEY, d.1916
PAGET, 1st Baron
QUEENBOROUGH,
GBE, 1861 - 1949

(2) 1921 = EDITH daughter of
William Starr MILLER,
of New York, d.1933

3 other sons and
8 daughters

FLORA
b & d
1896

Hon. (1) 1919 = OLIVE (2) 1925
CHARLES CECILIA
WINN, son of Leeds
of 2nd Lord Castle,
St. Oswald, Kent,
div 1925 1899 - 1974

= Arthur Thomas
Filmer WILSON
FILMER, div 1931

(3) 1931
= Sir Adrian BAILLIE,
6th Bt., div 1944

DOROTHY
WYNDHAM
PAGET,
1905 - 1960

Cmdt. Christian (1) 1945
MARTELL,
DFC, k 1945

AUDREY, (3) 1956
ELIZABETH,
1922 - 1991

ENID (2) 1947
Capt.
Comte Peter
Rollard LUCY, div
de la
POYPE, div

LOUISE, CAROL,
b.1923

CICILI 1947 = Capt.
Robert
EVANS,
DL, High
Sheriff of
Kent
1982
b.1928

(2) 1946 =
Alexander Ronan
NELSON, div 1956

Lt. Cmdr.
Peter
LUCY, div

(4) 1982
= Sir John
MUSKER

Gp Capt. Hon. = PAULINE (1) 1940
Edward WARD, KATHERINE,
div 1947 1920 - 1984

(3) 1960
= Boyd de
BROSSARD,
USA, div.

(2) 1948
Norman =
BUTLER
USA, div 1958

(4)
= Edward Lee
CAVE

Capt. Hon. Geoffrey (1) 1946
RUSSELL (now 4th
Lord Ampthill),
div 1971

SUSAN (2) 1972
MARY,
1923 - 2001

= Lt. Col. Edward
REMINGTON-
HOBBS, DSO, OBE

Sir GAWAINE 1966 = MARGOT,
GEORGE HOPE
BAILLIE, 7th Bt.,
b 1934
daughter of
Senator Louis
BEAUBIEN, of
Quebec

MARGOT, LIZA,
ADRIAN, b.1973 b.1969

SANDRA, = Timothy Baron (1) (2) Andrew
b.1949 J. HEISE. Ernest PAGET b.1953 MORSE
von
WEDEL,
div.

JAMES, Hon. = APRIL 1980
1948 - daughter of Paul
1969 DAVID RUSSELL, ARBON
b.1947

CHRISTABEL, DAISY,
b.1981 b.1983

CHRISTINE, (1) 1985 = Hon. (2) 1959 = CATHERINE LEFEBRE
daughter of John
O'DELL,
ANTHONY RUSSELL,
b.1952

WILLIAM,
b.1986

Charles (1) 1983 = Hon. (2) 1998 = Jonathan BOWLES
BURT, VANESSA, div.
b.1960

JAMES, EMMA,
b.1984 b.1986

Chapter Three

THE REBIRTH

The description by the agents of Fairfax Wykeham Martin when Leeds Castle was offered to let in 1925 was, in the manner of its kind, the truth but not the whole truth.

It said nothing about the need for some quite major repairs to the fabric of the building which was habitable – more or less – but entirely lacking the standard of comfort that the new owners expected of any home of theirs in the late 1920s.

Nevertheless, it suited the Wilson Filmers, certainly Mrs Wilson Filmer, very well. She was born in America and enjoyed dual British-American nationality, but she thought of herself as British and she wanted an English country home upon which she could exercise her undoubted creativity and taste. Leeds Castle was a challenge, and it was one she relished.

The report of the sale of the castle in *The Times* on 8 February, 1927, called it "the famous and very beautiful seat five miles from Maidstone ... with 3,200 acres, of which about one-tenth forms the park."

Although she came to the castle with a lot of ideas of her own, the new owner needed expert professional advice to help her achieve them. For that she employed first a Surrey-based architect called Owen Little. He designed the lodges for the entrances, all the work in the stable yard, and was responsible for much internal renovation for which he submitted designs to be approved by the French architectural designer Armand-Albert Rateau (1882-1938). Rateau was well-known in Paris before he came to Leeds Castle in 1927 and 1928 and had been involved in the building and restoration of major buildings in France and elsewhere, including America, Spain and Romania. She employed French and also Italian craftsmen, too, although all the internal demolition and much of the reconstruction work was done by local labour and British craftsmen.

It was, perhaps, natural enough that she should look to France for the expertise she needed. She had been educated in France, and inevitably she had absorbed elements of French culture and style. In the 1920s, Paris was still the cultural capital of the world and the very name carried resonances of chic and sophistication.

The Wilson Filmers had bought, with the castle, the entire 3,200 acre estate that went with it, including some 500 acres immediately surrounding the castle and about 750 acres of adjoining woodland. The rest was mostly farmed by tenants. The hamlet of Broomfield was wholly owned by the estate which also included individual properties in the neighbouring villages of Leeds and Hollingbourne.

The new owners lived in London while the work was going on to make the castle habitable. The main contractors for the restoration and renovation of the castle, the gatehouse and the gloriette were Keeble and Sons of Soho, London and the work of converting the Maiden's Tower from a brewhouse into bachelor apartments, and also work on the lodges, lodge gates and estate houses, was done by Jacob Long and Sons of Bath. Most of the work was actually carried out by sub-contractors.

The craftsman-foreman in charge of work on the castle itself was George Stammers, although one of the men most closely concerned with all that went on during that period and later was Joe Cooper, who had been at Leeds since 1911. He became a valued friend of Lady Baillie and it was very largely from his recollections that activities at the castle immediately after its acquisition by the new owners have been pieced together.

The late 1920s were difficult times for many workers. Skilled craftsmen had difficulty finding employment and the great deal of work that was needed to put Leeds Castle into order was a Godsend.

Although many of the workers were relatively local men, specialists from London were also employed, travelling down to Kent by train, in a special Southern Railway coach with a sign which said LEEDS CASTLE ONLY, and then by local bus service, staying in lodgings nearby during the week.

For an average wage of £3 a week, craftsmen were happy to

work on, when the natural light failed, with the aid of oil lamps and candles. One man recalled that when they broke off work for a meal, they were often visited by the castle rats that came to share their sandwiches. In fact, the whole castle was infested with rats until they had been successfully dealt with by rat-catchers.

Most of the men who came to work at the castle had never more than glimpsed the building through the trees that screened it from almost every approach. Their first impressions were not enthusiastic. Some of them, much later, remembered it as a grim ghost of a castle, empty, dark and sad. But they recognised it as a challenge to their different craftsmanships and many of them grew attached to the place as they saw their handiwork restoring it to life.

Before the building up could begin, though, there was a great deal to be torn down and that brought its own problems. Rain storms caused new damage to inadequately protected work under way. Floors and ceilings were ripped out and replaced at new levels and some of the external Kentish ragstone was replaced with sandstone. The tower on the corner of what is now the dining room nearest the Maiden's Tower was found to be out of alignment and had to be shored up with timber, windows in the turret dismantled, stone by numbered stone, and steel tie bars inserted to strain the turret back into position, so that one of the main water tanks could be installed in its top.

Gradually, the outline of the castle changed. The old tall chimneys were rebuilt and shortened, although this proved that the original builders knew a thing or two because the new chimneys made the fires smoke and a specialist – French again – was brought in to redesign the fireplaces, although Leeds lore claims that it was Joe Cooper who actually solved the problem.

At weekends, the castle's owner came with her daughters and her sister, Dorothy Paget, to inspect the progress of the work. Very often the only person able to converse freely with all the members of the multi-national workforce was the owner herself. In her absence, they had to manage as best they could to communicate in sign language, relying heavily upon the universal understanding of their various crafts. It must have been very much as it would have been when some of the great cathedrals, palaces and castles – including, no doubt, Leeds itself – were being built in mediaeval times.

Mains electricity was eventually brought from Maidstone, more than five miles away, and mains water from the A20, several hundred yards away, although the castle did have its own water supplied from a borehole in the park, which is still in use today.

Panelling for the principal drawing room, the first room on the left leading off the inner hall, was brought indirectly to Leeds from the great parlour of Thorpe Hall, near Peterborough, and the hundreds of small pieces were fitted together like a huge jigsaw puzzle. The fireplace came from there, too, and as a result, the room became known as the Thorpe Hall Room.

A door was made to connect the Thorpe Hall Room with what was the Library and is now the Yellow Drawing Room and the former small drawing room was opened to give access to an inner hall.

An oak staircase was replaced by Rateau with a very wide stone stairway with linenfold panelling above the stairwell. This has since been replaced again by the present one.

On each side of the central tower, major reconstruction at roof level enabled rooms to be built into the roof space to create bedrooms for female staff. Some of the young women who slept in them remembered them many years later as positively luxurious, compared with the servants' quarters in many of the big houses of the time, with carpeted floors, hot and cold running water and matching curtains and bedspreads.

A small outer hall led into the Great Hall (now the ladies' cloakroom and Heraldry Room), and entrances were cut to give access to these rooms. Doors were also made in the bases of the turrets in the Front Hall.

The Library (now the Yellow Drawing Room) became a breakfast room, all the shelving and cupboards being replaced by oak panelling and the Great Hall became the Library (now the Heraldry Room), where a Jacobean plaster ceiling and a large stone fireplace were installed. (The moulded ceiling and the floor are still as Lady Baillie knew them, but in other respects the room is quite different now.) Before the former small dining room became today's Library, it was a schoolroom for Lady Baillie's two daughters, Pauline and Susan. The large dining room was split into two unequal parts, becoming a stewards' room and a servants' hall.

On the upper floor, bedrooms were made smaller so that bathrooms could be installed between them, together with a clothes lobby for each pair of rooms.

Rateau used the existing outline of the gloriette to create a French gothic fantasy. The roof was largely removed; the chapel was dismantled and redesigned with linenfold oak panelling (since removed) to become a music room, from where recorded music was piped round the house; the mediaeval banqueting hall, which had been converted into three rooms, was restored to the original hall space, once the banqueting hall of Edward I, to become an evening drawing room known as the Saloon (now the Henry VIII Banqueting Hall). It had, at one end, a hidden spiral staircase, designed by Owen Little, by which Lady Baillie could descend from her own rooms on the first floor.

Here, stone-paved floors were removed and ebony flooring was laid on beams. An imposing chimneypiece was brought from France and installed by French craftsmen, as were oak doors which were hung in the newly fashioned stone doorways. A former larder became a reception room; the dairy, a card room; lower dairies were converted into cloakroom and boiler room: the house became one of the first in the country to have oil-fired heating. A still room and maids' room where the Queen's Room is now were altered to become a beamed dining room with a French tessellated floor and French wooden shutters, and a door was cut through the wall into the new dining room's serving room, once the Henry VI kitchen. The present Queen's Gallery was a writing room and the Queen's Bathroom was a card room where some pretty serious poker games were played at one period.

In the gloriette courtyard, a lath and plaster screen incorporated a newel staircase which was constructed in France and re-assembled by French carpenters. The newel post topped with the figure of a crusader was carved from a single tree trunk and looks authentically ancient.

On the upper floor of the gloriette, Lady Baillie had her bedroom and dressing room, with French parquet flooring and French fireplaces. A billiard room became Lady Baillie's boudoir and, later, a bedroom for her son, Sir Gawaine. Now it is the Seminar Room.

Later, Sir Adrian Baillie had a sunny apartment in the gloriette, with a marble bathroom. The apartment was subsequently converted into a boudoir and it is now the Catherine of Aragon bedroom.

Elsewhere, the servants' hall became the kitchen; part of the butler's bedroom became a walk-in safe; the ivy tower, which alone of the mediaeval building remains at its full height, was re-roofed. The Maiden's Tower, which had been used as a brewhouse, had to be stabilised and repointed while the inside was completely redesigned by Rateau so that very little of the Tudor interior remained. It was used by bachelor guests and children and also for staff bedrooms, although at different times part of it was also used as a cinema and a drawing room.

Garages were built around a quadrangle to the north of the 17th century barn (now the Fairfax Hall), which was re-roofed. A laundry (now offices) was built behind the garages while stables for about thirty horses were created out of the buildings around the farmyard, east of the barn.

This initial stage of the work took three years and was not without its tragedy. These were days before metal scaffolding, when all lifting was done by rope-and-pulley manpower, and as some interior beams were being removed in the Maiden's Tower, one fell and a workman was killed.

The work created a great deal of rubbish that had to be got rid of, too, and a bridge was specially built across the moat to take a light railway on which to carry away rubbish and bring in new materials. It was quite a feat of engineering ingenuity in itself but it did save a lot of time and trouble.

Oak timber for the rebuilding work was brought in from all over Europe. Each had its own different characteristics and all had to be treated so that it matched, as did similarly imported doors and other structural woodwork.

While the work was in progress, a temporary works office was set up in a shed that was actually afloat on pontoons on the moat. It was from here that the men were paid and on one occasion, a dropped pay packet fell through the pontoon planks into the water. One of the younger men dived in to recover it but the notes had floated away and the men in the queue immediately had a whip-round for the unfortunate loser.

Gradually, the old castle, which had undergone equally fundamental transformations before in its long history, assumed its latest configuration. There is never an end to the work that needs to be done on a building like Leeds Castle and each new owner who accepts responsibility for its upkeep also wants to adapt it to meet evolving standards of domestic comfort and convenience and reflect his or her own architectural and decorative tastes.

By 1928, then, what we can now recognise as the Lady Baillie influence had been stamped on the general appearance of the building. Now it was time to create the life-style that would complement the character of this unique country house in the heart of Kent.

Chapter Four

MOVING IN

During those first few years, large sums of money were spent on Leeds Castle. The basic structure was completely renovated and the gloriette was gutted and rebuilt internally. The work was still going on when the family moved in and it continued for some time after that.

The park, which had been neglected and become overgrown, was cleared and work began on the gardens with their greenhouses. The wood garden was created, bordered by the Len streams, and llamas and zebras were introduced to graze freely in the grounds, while parakeets and storks added character to the lakes and the gardens.

Although Olive Wilson Filmer continued to spend most of her time at the family's London home, she, together with her two daughters, Pauline and Susan Winn, aged eight and five respectively, and her sister, Dorothy Paget, moved into the castle in June 1928. Pauline and Susan grew up at the castle, where they had their own schoolroom and tutors.

It was a great place for youngsters to grow up in. Both girls inherited the family love of riding and they could ride their ponies freely in the castle grounds. There was a whole Great Outdoors on their doorstep to be explored and to provide a perfect playground for themselves and their friends. When it was hot, they swam in the moat – children are less squeamish and often hardier than their elders! – before the heated swimming pool was built in the late 1930s.

To the girls, and to some of the family friends who visited it, the castle had a ghostly air about it. The children, of course, relished it but on one occasion their mother, armed with only an electric torch, set out to tour every part of the house by herself, just to prove that there were no resident ghosts. Whether or not she proved any such thing, it certainly demonstrated that she did not lack courage.

Dorothy Paget shared the family love of horses but her enthusiasm turned to race-horses. For a time after the move to Kent, she rented Mote Park, Maidstone, where she stabled her horses. She hoped to buy land nearby for stables of her own but Maidstone council wanted it for the development that became the Shepway Estate and so Dorothy's horses were stabled for a time at Leeds Castle. The horse that was to win the Grand National and five Cheltenham Gold Cups for her, Golden Miller, was stabled there before she moved to her own stables at Elsenham, where she bred such distinguished horses as the 1943 Derby winner Straight Deal and many others.

So, once again, Leeds Castle resumed its role of family country home and it was not long before it began to earn a reputation for the hospitality it offered to weekend guests. In September 1928 the Daily Mail carried a story which described Leeds Castle as the perfect place to spend a weekend and where the Hon Mrs Wilson Filmer and her husband had been giving "one of their usual house parties".

The report outlined some of the attractions for guests – fishing for giant pike in the moat, playing golf on the private golf course, riding – "and, if he happens to be invited for the same weekend as yourself, you can listen to Rex Evans singing his latest songs".

Listening to Rex Evans was, evidently, something of a special treat. He was a singer with an international reputation although the writer added that his songs were "not as daring as some of those sung at Leeds Castle over the weekend".

These "daring" songs were written by American Cole Porter and earned the comment: "I doubt whether they would ever pass the Censor over here."

At this time, the same Daily Mail writer said, the castle itself was "still in splints". He went on to say that thousands of pounds had been spent, but hundreds of workmen were still employed on the renovations and extensions which, it was hoped, would be completed by Christmas.

It was after this article's publication that the curtain of

discretion was drawn across activities at the castle and public interest in events there was fed by rumour rather than by report. Inevitably, that very discretion encouraged gossip locally. One former junior housemaid who joined the castle staff in her teens, recalled many years later her grandmother's consternation when she learned that her grand-daughter was working "in that den of iniquity".

The lady herself was unable to recall any behaviour that warranted such a condemnation, unless it was the gambling and drinking that went on, about which she could only say: "I didn't really know very much about that at all. The staff took all that very much for granted."

This was, of course, the early Thirties, when the prevailing mood of the Twenties could still be summed up in the words of the popular Cole Porter song, *Anything Goes*. It was a time when young people generally scorned the moral and behavioural standards of earlier decades. Much the same kind of "revolution" would take place again, in the Swinging Sixties, on a broader and even less inhibited scale.

Inevitably, reports seeped out of ill-defined "goings on" at the castle. One young woman, Pamela Digby, a friend of Pauline Winn and a regular visitor to Leeds Castle, became something of a protégé of Pauline's mother, Lady Baillie, whom Pamela cultivated for as long as the association suited her. Pamela married Randolph Churchill in October 1939 thus becoming Winston Churchill's daughter-in-law before she became Mrs Pamela Harriman. Her biographers characterised the castle as the training ground for her later career as an irrepressible socialite and "the country's greatest courtesan".

She and Averell Harriman were guests at Leeds Castle while they were still married to other partners but, according to Lady Mary Dunn, friend and one-time landlady of Pamela and the source of that particular report, it was probably only once, because Pamela Churchill, as she still was, was notoriously indiscreet, and indiscretion was a trait that was not condoned at the castle.

Although Lady Baillie earned a reputation as a considerate and lavish hostess, her insistence that she should not be the subject of any publicity of any kind ensured that there is no evidence that the partying at Leeds was very different from that which could have been enjoyed in many houses of the same kind at that period.

One event that was permitted to be noticed by the local Press was the sports gala day that was held at the castle in aid of the Kent Playing Fields Association on Saturday, 27 July 1929. According to a report published in the *Kent Messenger* the following week, upward of 5,000 people attended to watch the golf competition, lawn tennis exhibition and other events and to take a rare opportunity of simply wandering through the grounds and gardens.

The paper reported: "So dense was the stream of cars entering the grounds during the afternoon that traffic on the Ashford Road was held up for a considerable length of time. The number of cars parked is estimated at between two and three thousand."

The report detailed the more noteworthy ticket holders, including the Marchioness of Ormonde, Lord and Lady Cornwallis, Mr and Mrs [James] Campbell Bannerman [of Hunton Court, nephew of the late Prime Minister, Sir Henry Campbell Bannerman], and the Ven E H Hardcastle, Archdeacon of Canterbury. The nine-hole golf competition attracted about 30 pairs of players, including some of the best-known players of the day. But the exhibition tennis, "staged on well-sheltered hard courts where the surrounding green banks formed a natural amphitheatre affording a view to thousands of onlookers" (to quote the local reporter), lacked three South African players who were called abroad at the last minute and the famous young English player, H W Austin, who had had to go to America earlier in the week and could not take part.

At the end of the day, Mrs Wilson Filmer and her daughters, Pauline and Susan, were thanked by the Association's executive committee chairman, Mr R L Murray Lawes, for lending the castle grounds and for giving the cup that was presented to the winners of the golf competition.

It was obviously regarded as a very successful day and something of a social event at which to be seen. The total proceeds were reported to be £733.

Lady Baillie's London home was now 45 Upper Grosvenor Street and she and her new husband spent most of their time there, driving down to Leeds Castle at weekends to entertain guests.

Lady Baillie built a reputation for the kind of hospitality that put her among the notable hostesses of her day. Her husband introduced political friends to Leeds Castle, including the already experienced Parliamentarian and Government Chief Whip, David Margesson and, later, the up-and-coming Geoffrey Lloyd. Both became her life-long friends and very influential members of the Leeds Castle ménage.

David Margesson was 42 when he first came to Leeds Castle in 1932. He had married an American heiress, Frances Leggett, in 1916 by whom he had a son and two daughters. The marriage was dissolved in 1940. During the 1914-18 war, he served with the 11th Hussars and won a Military Cross before he left the army with the rank of captain – by which the castle staff always referred to him. He was first elected to the House of Commons as Conservative MP for the Upton division of West Ham in 1922, but it was as MP for Rugby from 1924-42 that he made his reputation.

He joined the Whips' Office in 1924 as an Assistant Whip and by 1931 he was the Government Chief Whip, an office he held from 1931 until 1940, under four Prime Ministers, Ramsay MacDonald, Stanley Baldwin, Neville Chamberlain and Winston Churchill. Under Churchill, he was Parliamentary Secretary to the Treasury and Chief Government Whip jointly with former Labour Chief Whip Sir Charles Edwards, and for eighteen months (1940-1942) he was Secretary of State for War. In his *Second World War Diary*, Hugh Dalton said David Margesson was considered as a possible leader of the Conservative Party in the House of Commons in 1942. He was raised to the peerage as the first Viscount Margesson of Rugby in March 1942 after which he spent another twenty years as a fairly inconspicuous member of the House of Lords. He died in 1965.

Over six feet tall, soldierly, lean, dark and strikingly handsome, always an elegant figure, he enjoyed the admiration of women of all ages, although he had a reputation for imposing a forceful personality from the Whips' office where he could be dictatorial, even ruthless, and a rigid disciplinarian. He cultivated contacts and hoarded inside information so that he became one of the most powerful men in the country, but he was a great mixer and instinctively diplomatic, skilled at pouring oil on troubled waters whenever differences of opinion threatened to become acrimonious or relationships strained and he was widely respected and generally well-liked. His intimate knowledge of the private and professional lives of every politician and many other "top" people, too, meant that at informal gatherings he could gossip wittily and he was a genial and entertaining guest at any party.

His bedroom at the castle was the Yellow Room on the first floor of the gloriette.

Geoffrey Lloyd first stayed at Leeds Castle in 1934, when he was 32, having won the Ladywood division of Birmingham for the Conservatives at the second try in 1931. A quietly-spoken but entertaining bachelor, he had already been private secretary to Sir Samuel Hoare, Secretary of State for Air, from 1926 to 1929 and private secretary to Stanley Baldwin from 1929 to 1931. He was Baldwin's Parliamentary Private Secretary when Baldwin was Lord President of the Council from November 1931 until June 1935 and when he was Prime Minister from June to November 1935.

Geoffrey Lloyd was younger than Lady Baillie but he quickly became a permanent feature of the Leeds Castle household. At one time, servants' gossip asserted that he wanted to marry Lady Baillie's elder daughter, Pauline, but in fact he remained a lifelong bachelor. He was successively Secretary for Mines (1939-1940), Secretary for Petroleum (1940-1942) and Parliamentary Secretary for Petroleum in the Ministry of Fuel and Power (1942-

1945). He was Chairman of the Oil Control Board (1939-1945), Minister in Charge of the Petroleum Warfare Department (1940-1945), Minister of Information (1945), Governor of the BBC (1946-1949), Minister of Fuel and Power (1951-1955) and Minister of Education (1957-1959). He was created Baron Geoffrey-Lloyd of Broomfield in 1974 and was Chairman of the Leeds Castle Foundation from then until his death in 1984.

He was a polished charmer and members of the castle staff who knew him in later years described him as "a dear" and "a very nice man". In the 1930s he was young, ambitious and well aware of the power that knowledge brought. He became an avid collector and astute analyst of information of all kinds and in the course of his long political career he became one of the best-informed men in the country.

Sir Adrian Baillie was an all-round sportsman, good at tennis and better at golf, who had a good singing voice, too; a pleasant, rather easy-going man who was happy to leave most of the organising of the social and domestic life of the castle to his wife. He spent much of his time at Polkemmet, his Scottish family home and after their son, Gawaine, was born in 1934, Sir Adrian and Lady Baillie drifted apart. Increasingly, it was to David Margesson and Geoffrey Lloyd that she looked for advice and support.

The two men were friends of both Sir Adrian and Lady Baillie and remained so for about 10 years. They had their own rooms at Leeds Castle and between them they seemed to fill a role in her life that was, perhaps, never filled in marriage. The "Very Important People" to whom Margaret, Duchess of Argyll, referred in her autobiography certainly included David Margesson and Geoffrey Lloyd but although momentous political decisions may have been made at Leeds, whether Lady Baillie played any significant part in reaching them, or ever wanted to, is open to considerable doubt.

Pamela Harriman's biographer, Christopher Ogden, described Leeds Castle in the early 1930s as "the most stimulating salon in Britain" with glamorous friends and international visitors at intimate weekend parties. In her book *Reflected Glory*, Sally Bedell Smith judged the "Leeds set" to rival and even to surpass Nancy Astor's Cliveden Set in diversity and talent, although the two "sets" were different and the veil of discretion lay much more thickly over Leeds.

It may well have been Lady Baillie's aversion to personal publicity of any kind, coupled with the company she kept and the reputation she earned for absolute discretion, that enabled rumour to attach so much political weight to what went on there.

But the fact is, none of the leading figures in the Leeds Castle household left any autobiographical records of life at the castle throughout the fifty years of Lady Baillie's ownership. Posterity has only the memories of family members, friends and castle staff from which to deduce what it will.

Chapter Five

THE PARTY YEARS

Every now and again a decade seems to startle Time itself out of its natural rhythm and make it jump, so that it carries on a little ahead of where it would otherwise have been. The Sixties were rather like that. So, too, were the Twenties. Both brought sudden changes in standards of social behaviour for later decades to adjust to.

But, in ways that the Seventies did not, the Thirties spanned a troubled decade. It began with the maelstrom of the Depression which, although its effects were felt much more severely at some levels of society than at others, nevertheless put something of a damper on the overall atmosphere; and it ended with the increasing international tensions that finally exploded into the Second World War in 1939.

Even so, despite the many domestic difficulties, England in the Thirties seemed a haven of relative stability in a Europe seething with political strife. Here, there remained a clearly defined class distinction which was, on the whole, accepted unquestioningly at all levels. Fascism and Nazism were widely regarded as a timely challenge to continental Communism rather than as any sort of threat to Britain's capitalist democracy and notwithstanding events in Spain and the increasingly imperialistic aspirations of the Italian and German dictators, Mussolini and Hitler, the prevailing mood in England, especially among the better-off, favoured the status quo, appeasement and "peace in our time".

A few "warmongers" like Winston Churchill advocated military opposition to the dictators, but it was not until 1935 that they began to be taken very seriously and throughout the period most people strove to maintain whatever normality they were used to. That was as true of the Leeds Castle "set" as of any other.

Margaret, Duchess of Argyll, who was a long-time friend of Lady Baillie and who visited the castle on several occasions, recalled the 1930s as "a severely moral period", when there was a strong reaction against the decadence of the 1920s and life, although frivolous, was very "proper". She described the week-end house parties at Leeds as luxurious and amusing, seldom with less than thirty guests.

Sir Adrian and Lady Baillie often travelled down to Leeds separately in their own cars to meet their guests for the weekend parties. Lady Baillie's lifelong love of the cinema ensured that guests included some of the most celebrated film stars of their day, and members of the Royal Family came from time to time, too.

Among the many guests who enjoyed weekends at Leeds were Edward, Prince of Wales (later Duke of Windsor), who came with Mrs Simpson, and Prince George (for whom the title of Duke of Kent was revived by his father, King George V, in October 1934) and Princess Marina of Greece, later to become Duchess of Kent. Others included Queen Marie of Romania, her daughter, Princess Ileana and her son-in-law the Archduke Anton of Austria; Alfonso XIII of Spain and the Russian Grand Duke Dimitri Pavolovich, one of the conspirators who had plotted the assassination of "*Mad Monk*" Rasputin in 1916.

Other guests included Sir Alfred Beit, Bt, the art patron and collector, and a distinguished array of Ambassadors, Ministers and Members of Parliament of all political parties including Nazi Germany's Ambassador to Britain, Joachim von Ribbentrop, who met the British Foreign Secretary, Anthony Eden, at Leeds.

Film stars included Douglas Fairbanks Senior and Junior, Frederick March, Charlie Chaplin, Eroll Flynn and his wife, Lili Damita, Robert Taylor, James Stewart, and Gertrude Lawrence. Other guests were the Woolworths heiress Barbara Hutton, one of whose several husbands was British-born film star Cary Grant, whom she married in July 1942, and Ian Fleming, later to become famous as the author of the James Bond novels.

One man who became a great friend of Lady Baillie was the singer Richard Tauber. He had recently married the actress Diana Napier when they first met Sir Adrian and Lady Baillie and he had his own piano brought to the castle where he spent many hours entertaining his hostess and her friends, accompanying himself or being accompanied by one of the others on the piano. He also greatly entertained housemaids and other members of the staff when he sang in his bath while they went about their morning duties.

Interestingly, in October 1935, the Richard Tauber film *Heart's Desire* was given its world premier at the gala opening of The Ritz Cinema in Maidstone, the rebuilt People's Picture Palace in Pudding Lane, supported by the first Mickey Mouse film in colour, *The Band Concert*.

Lady Baillie was one of the four signatories of Tauber's naturalisation papers when he adopted British nationality after he was forced out of his native Austria by the Nazis because his father was Jewish. After he died, of lung cancer, Lady Baillie invited his widow to stay at Leeds Castle while his somewhat tangled affairs were being sorted out. Her story of her life with Richard, *My Heart and I*, published in 1959, was dedicated to Coonie, the nickname by which Lady Baillie was known to her friends.

Weekend guests usually arrived on Friday evening or between about eight and ten o'clock on Saturday morning. Most of them came by car, but occasionally someone flew in by chartered plane, especially if they were abroad at the time, landing at nearby Broomfield.

Hospitality at Leeds Castle was unstinted. After breakfast, there was golf, tennis, squash in the castle's own court (now the Dog Collar Museum), croquet, boating or skating on the moat depending upon the season, and riding. There were more than four hundred acres of splendid parkland in which informal picnics could sometimes be enjoyed.

Dinner, which was normally arranged for eight o'clock but was often delayed for an hour by the non-appearance of the hostess, was a lively meal, spiced with good conversation and gossip, after which, as an alternative to cards, sometimes the carpet would be rolled back from the ebony-floored saloon, now the Banqueting Hall, and there was dancing to gramophone music relayed from the adjoining room (now the Chapel). Alternatively, there might be a film show or the company would be entertained by one of their number.

Some of the male guests stayed in the Maiden's Tower, separated from the main building by the castle's inner bailey, which did not bode well for those who hoped to take part in the "good deal of bed hopping" that went on after dark, according to one source quoted in Christopher Ogden's biography of Pamela Harriman, *Life of the Party*.

In a later Harriman biography, *Reflected Glory*, Sally Bedell Smith wrote that Lady Baillie issued weekend invitations with the care of a casting director, ensuring a mix of bright and decorative people who included politicians, actors, artists, film and stage stars, but most of the weekend parties were made up, week after week, of the same friends, with an occasional distinguished guest or two.

Pamela Harriman herself described Olive Baillie as "relatively restrained in behaviour compared with many of her much more notorious contemporaries".

"Above all," she said, "she was discreet, which many were not. She didn't need to seduce rich men. Her special aphrodisiac was power."

As a hostess, Lady Baillie had the enviable knack of making all her visitors feel at home and they had the full run of the castle while they were there. But although she entertained a great many people, she kept her circle of close friends relatively small.

Weekends at Leeds were, in fact, very much like the many other country house weekends at that time. These were a favourite source of inspiration for many authors and playwrights, including one of the best-known of them all, Noel Coward, despite his own self-confessed aversion to country house parties.

In his autobiography, *Past Conditional*, he wrote: "To me, the very idea of a round of country house visits is anathema. I would rather stay at an hotel than in other people's houses … unless, of course, they happen to belong to close friends with whom I can relax. I do not care for the obligation of having to be considerate to other people's servants, nor do I care to experiment with other people's ideas of comfort, which are so often widely dissimilar

Lady Baillie on the day of her marriage to Sir Adrian Baillie in 1931.

Sir Adrian and Lady Baillie's son, Gawaine, was born 1934 in Scotland.

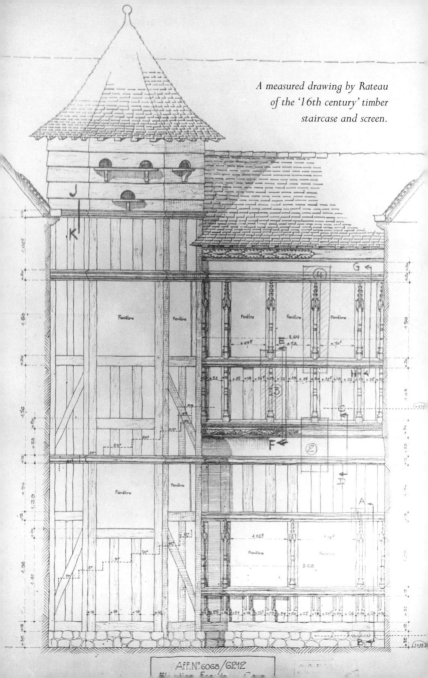

A measured drawing by Rateau of the '16th century' timber staircase and screen.

Aff. Nº 6068 / 6212

Italian and French carvers working on the beams.

Rateau's bridge over Broomfield Road for the use of golfers.

The temporary bridge and railway track over the moat to the sally port workshops.

Opposite right: The timber frame of the spiral staircase in the early stages of construction.

The Writing Room, now the Chapel.

The Castle was purchased in 1927 for £180,000, with £100,000 necessary for restoration. This winter photograph shows building work and the south front clad in scaffolding.

Lady Baillie's Dining Room in the late 1920s, now the Queen's Room.

THE PARTY YEARS

Photo courtesy of Mirror Syndication International.

'Certainly, the film star David Niven (left), seems to have had no reservations about accepting invitations to Leeds. He was a great friend of Errol Flynn and the two of them were guests at Leeds more than once. Niven made his special mark with the staff when he deserted fellow guests to play cards with some of the servants in the hall.'

Signatures from the Leeds Castle Visitors' Book ~ luminaries here include from top: Prime Minister Anthony Eden and Errol Flynn who added the date April 17th 1937.

Glamorous guests ~ clockwise from left: Douglas Fairbanks Jnr. with Academy Award and Loretta Young, Errol Flynn, Noel Coward and Douglas Fairbanks and Mary Pickford. Photos courtesy of PA Photos.

George Howard and Friends on the tennis pavilion verandah, 1928.

Madame Southiere, Lady Baillie's French governess, and later governess to Lady Baillie's daughters Pauline and Susan.

THE LIBRARY

Lady Baillie used it first as a schoolroom where her daughters received their early education. In 1938 Stéphane Boudin redesigned it after a late 17th century model.

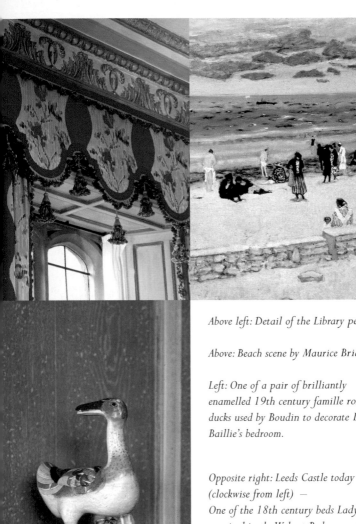

Above left: Detail of the Library pelmet.

Above: Beach scene by Maurice Brianchon.

Left: One of a pair of brilliantly enamelled 19th century famille rose ducks used by Boudin to decorate Lady Baillie's bedroom.

Opposite right: Leeds Castle today (clockwise from left) — One of the 18th century beds Lady Baillie acquired in the Walnut Bedroom; stylish 1920s fixtures and fittings in her Bathroom by Rateau and the opulent blue decoration created by Boudin in her Bedroom.

Photos: Peter Smith

The Home Guard (Hollingbourne Battalion), during WWII, pictured in the stableyard of Leeds Castle.

VADs (Voluntary Aid Detachments) at Leeds Castle in the 1940s with Lady Baillie (inset), seated next to Col. Boyd, RAMC.

The stableyard of Leeds Castle in the 1940s.

Leeds Castle today.

Peter Taylor was employed as Lady Baillie's bird keeper from 1953 until her death in 1974; seen here at the opening of the new Aviary in 1988.

Lady Baillie's favourite bird — the toucan.

Scarlet macaw.

One of a pair of tame whooper swans resident at the castle.

The Cedar Pond at Leeds Castle.

A variety of wild birds feed at the edge of the Moat: Coot, Jackdaws, Mallard ducks and a Canada goose.

Black swans on the Leeds Castle moat.

Lady Baillie at Leeds Castle in the 1960s with her German shepherd dog Elsa.

from my own."

Presumably, he came to include Lady Baillie among those close friends with whom he could relax because the estate's former resident agent, John Money, who began his long association with the castle in 1950, recalled sitting in the saloon and listening to Noel Coward, among others, playing the Steinway concert grand piano, which was subsequently replaced by a smaller instrument.

Certainly, the film star David Niven seems to have had no reservations about accepting invitations to Leeds. He was a great friend of Errol Flynn and the two of them were guests at Leeds more than once. Niven made his special mark with the staff when he deserted fellow guests to play cards with some of the servants in the hall.

As well as Leeds Castle, the Baillies also had the family home at Polkemmet in Scotland, where they spent part of every year for the shooting. In addition, they rented various properties in London, including a house in Grosvenor Square that is now part of the site of the American Embassy, and a villa in France. They had a yacht too, and after the war there was a house in the Bahamas. Later London homes included a house in Chesterfield Street and, finally, Lowndes House in Lowndes Place.

Lady Baillie was an equally generous hostess in London as she was in Kent. The coming out dance given for her elder daughter, Pauline (Popsy) Winn, in May 1938 was among the most lavish of the season. Pauline, at 18, was one of the brightest of the season's bright young things and at the dance, which was held at the house on the corner of Grosvenor Square and Upper Brook Street, food was served in a silver and gold dining room set up in a floodlit garden, where Richard Tauber sang.

A contemporary report described how every room in the house glowed with candlelight and there were two ballrooms, one for traditional dancing and the other for the more modern dances, like The Big Apple and The Lambeth Walk.

Every summer, the Baillies went to the Côte d'Azur where Lady Baillie gambled enthusiastically, while her husband enjoyed the rather less sedentary pleasures of the local nightclubs.

At home, it was Lady Baillie's normal practice to rise very late in the morning, having already completed much of the day's work in her own room. Consequently, lunch was a very irregular meal. But on a Monday morning, after a weekend at Leeds, she sometimes left for London quite early, in her chauffeur-driven Rolls-Royce, usually accompanied by her secretary.

It was in 1933 that Lady Baillie first met the man who was to have the greatest influence on the castle's interior decor, after Armand-Albert Rateau. He was the French designer, Stéphane Boudin (1888-1967), who bestowed his talents on some of the most beautiful homes all over the world. The American-born diarist of the 1930s and 1940s, Chips Channon, called him the greatest decorator in the world.

Boudin went to work for the world-famous interior decorating firm of Jansen, on the rue Royale in Paris, in 1923, when he was 35 and had already made a name for himself. During a brilliant career, his many illustrious clients included the Duke and Duchess of Windsor and Jacqueline Kennedy, for whom he redecorated parts of The White House.

From 1936 until he died in 1967 Boudin collaborated with Lady Baillie on renovation and improvements at Leeds Castle. From architectural detail and the acquisition of furniture to the colours of the flowers in the arrangements with which the house was always filled, nothing was done before he had been consulted. Although Lady Baillie always made the decisions, so well did their tastes coincide that there was rarely any kind of disagreement.

Together, they introduced fashionable English and French furniture, much of it good reproduction eighteenth century Louis XV and Louis XVI. Each room was given an individual colour scheme and character and a Leeds Castle "special" was the robin's egg blue used in the dining room, with its complementary green and red Chinese porcelain.

Like Lady Baillie herself, Boudin was always striving for an elusive perfection and workmen were sometimes required to carry out work over and over again before he was satisfied with the result. It was he who advised about where furniture and ornaments should be placed in order to achieve the best view of them from adjoining rooms, so that each room became part of a greater whole.

With Boudin's help, much of the castle's interior was redesigned, particularly in the new castle. The former breakfast room became the Yellow Drawing Room, with an Inigo Jones style neo-palladian chimneypiece and walls covered in yellow damask. Windows were lowered to open on to a balcony leading down to the lawn.

Lady Baillie's first library, designed by Rateau, in the old hall, was dismantled and the space used to create a staff dining room and a sitting room, again rearranged in 1975, when the Heraldry Room was created.

The main staircase installed by Rateau was replaced with the present stone staircase designed by Boudin and on the east side of the house Boudin adapted the former schoolroom into a panelled Library with double doors leading into the Dining Room.

Staff learned to dread what became known as "*Boudin weekends*" because they were occasions when the whole place was liable to be turned upside down. Furniture was brought in and taken out, rearranged or moved from one room to another, and staff were on call virtually twenty-four hours a day in order to achieve the desired results in the time available. It all made a lot of extra work, although there was never any doubt that the results were worthwhile.

Boudin and Lady Baillie became close friends and worked well together. His influence is best seen today in her bedroom, where he used his special techniques to make new panelling look old, bringing out the grain in new wood by scouring it with steel brushes before it was painted, and in the Yellow Drawing Room, the Library and the Dining Room. There have been no major changes, only redecoration in the same colour schemes, to the castle since about 1946.

In 1939 the castle swimming pool was completed. It was, like so much else at Leeds, the last word in amenities of its kind in this country, open-air but heated and with a switch that enabled waves to be made. An adjoining cocktail bar was embellished with a mural entitled *Boys Will Be Boys* which showed Neville Chamberlain skating on a pond covered in thin ice and surrounded by statues of buxom ladies being removed, one by one. Each one was labelled, respectively *The Rape of Austria, The Rape of Czechoslovakia, The Rape of Abyssinia*. Hiding in the background were two naughty urchins, recognisable as Hitler and Goering, and Duff Cooper and Winston Churchill stood looking on.

It illustrated with wry humour the unlovely end to which the tumultuous decade was drawing when, in May 1939, the author H V Morton, having decided that war was inevitable and anxious for a last glimpse of pre-war England, journeyed into Kent at the beginning of his tour of the country that he chronicled in *I Saw Two Englands*. One of his stops was at Leeds Castle which, he noted, was open to the public only once or twice a year.

He commented: "Leeds Castle is unknown, except to those who have enjoyed the hospitality of Lady Baillie …"

He paid his half a crown (say twelve-and-a-half pence) entrance fee, which was in fact a donation to charity, and drove his car into the park where he saw "a castle that might have been created by Tennyson or Walter Scott…. It is enormous. When the sun is shining, the effect of the stone is striking: it is as white as marble.

I sat on the grass and thanked God that Leeds Castle does not belong to me. To have to live in such a colossal place, and to maintain there a great pack of retainers … is just my idea of purgatory.

I thought how remarkable it is in these days, when incomes can pay more than ten shillings in the pound income tax and people are less inclined than ever to assume responsibility, that anyone can be found who loves this old castle sufficiently to keep life within its walls."

Guided by a member of the castle staff, he toured the living rooms before returning to the highway and heading for Canterbury, like a gate-crasher slipping away from a party that was almost over.

Chapter Six

THE STAFF

The "great pack of retainers" that H V Morton was so glad not to have to maintain was perhaps not quite as great as he might have imagined. Pre-war, there were about forty permanent members of staff, indoors and out, at the castle and, after the war, rather less than that.

Apart from the "office staff", such as the agent and secretaries, the indoor staff normally included the house steward, butler, under-butler and three footmen, plus a nursery footman, hall boy and odd-job man. The chef had five kitchen maids and the housekeeper was in charge of eight housemaids.

Out of doors, six or seven gardeners worked under the head gardener, and there were various other groundsmen, chauffeurs, laundry staff, grooms, gamekeepers – not forgetting "Old Dan'l" (no-one seemed to know him by any other name) and his carthorse, Charlie, who carried the rubbish bins to the lodge gates for collection and did various other odd jobs around the grounds.

Staff acted as guides to visitors whenever the castle and its grounds were open to the public, as they were once or twice a year in support of such charities as the Gardeners' Benevolent Fund and the National Gardens Scheme for District Nurses.

Senior footmen also acted as valets to gentlemen guests who arrived unaccompanied by servants of their own while the housekeeper and senior housemaids looked after the lady guests who did not bring maids with them.

Most of the more junior members of staff, such as the housemaids (some of whom began working at the castle at the age of fifteen), saw very little of Lady Baillie, even by accident, since they were under instructions to make themselves inconspicuous (by disappearing temporarily into a convenient cupboard if necessary) if they happened to be caught at their work when their employer approached.

But long after they left the castle, they were almost unanimous in their acknowledgement that Lady Baillie was a good employer – even if she did find it difficult to understand that prompt payment of wages was a matter of some consequence to servants earning little more than £20 a year, all found. It was not unknown for staff to have to wait up to three months for their wages because their employer did not always appreciate the urgency of the need for such relatively small sums of money. However, many of the guests were generous with tips, which could amount to as much as ten shillings (50p) for valeting. Junior staff shared pooled tips after their seniors had taken their own share.

The original butler was Frank Bell, who was followed by Mr Boucher and, finally, Mr Borrett and there was a succession of housekeepers too.

Some of the unmarried male staff had their rooms over the archway leading out of the stable yard where the Fairfax Hall now is, and today's courtyard shop was formerly a staff clubroom and hostel which provided a recreational facility for the considerable community that served the castle. Open to both men and women, there was a bar, and billiards and darts tournaments were organised at which the castle staff entertained visiting competitors from surrounding village pubs and other local organisations. Some of the trophies won by castle employees are still exhibited proudly in cabinets and on mantelpieces in cottages throughout the neighbourhood.

Although weekends were hectic for all the staff, life at Leeds Castle for the servants was by no means all work and no play. They had a half-day off every week and every other Sunday off, and either morning or afternoon off on alternate Sundays. They made up coach parties to go to dances in the neighbouring villages or to the seaside and when the owner was not in residence, staff duties were relatively light and they were free to use the golf course and tennis courts during their leisure time.

Christmas at Leeds Castle was memorable. Every year, except during the war, there was a big family party to which all the children of the staff and estate workers were invited. It took gardeners several days to decorate the rooms and the stairs and a big Christmas tree was set up and decorated. The top of the tree was trimmed to make it seem that it went up through the ceiling.

The children and their mothers were collected from their homes on the estate by lorry, and taken to one of the castle rooms, which was festooned with balloons and giant swags of paper chains. There was tea, with sandwiches, cakes, jellies and ice cream and fruit, and a big log fire. Later on they would be joined by the men who worked on the estate.

There were games or an entertainment of some kind, perhaps a magician, in another room and then the eagerly awaited arrival of Father Christmas. On at least one occasion, the children crowded to the windows to watch Father Christmas being rowed towards them across the moat and then, after he had disappeared from view below, he re-appeared from the big fireplace, having apparently made his traditional entry by way of the chimney. The children loved it.

There was a present for every child, who had been asked in advance what he or she wanted. They usually got it, whether it was a doll or roller skates or a football, handed to them by Lady Baillie herself or one of her daughters, assisted by Sir Adrian or Lord Queenborough and sometimes by a senior member of staff. Finally, the tree would be stripped of the chocolate baubles, which were then handed round.

Long afterwards, many of the children retained happy memories of those Christmas parties at the castle.

For their parents there were Christmas gifts of money, adjusted annually according to Lady Baillie's judgment of what was deserved, and handed over during the afternoon of Christmas Eve. There was also a brace of rabbits or a joint of pork for everyone.

On New Year's Eve, Sir Adrian honoured his family's Scottish tradition by gathering the staff together and dispensing punch for them to join him in a toast to the New Year. There was always a New Year's ball for the staff, too, at which Sir Adrian led the dancing with the housekeeper and Lady Baillie danced with the butler. The following day was always regarded as an "easy" day for staff, most of whom had had a late night.

Christmas at Leeds Castle during the 1930s could still illuminate the memories of those who experienced it sixty years later when, with a sad shake of the head, they could only suppose "we shall never see their like again".

The Baillie heir, Gawaine, was born in 1934 at Polkemmet in Scotland amid much rejoicing. His birth was announced with the lighting of bonfires and at Leeds there was a staff ball, with the whole lower part of the house taken over by the staff for eating, drinking, dancing and card-playing. All the staff were invited to the christening at Leeds church, where Prince George, later to become Duke of Kent, was one of the baby's Godfathers.

When, in 1935, King George V and Queen Mary celebrated their Silver Jubilee, all the Leeds villagers were invited to the castle grounds where there was a fun fair, and there were sweets and ice cream and a commemorative bone china mug with a picture of the castle on it for all the children.

In the following January, when the king died, as many of the staff as wished to go were taken by coach to Westminster Hall to see the late king lying in state, sweeping past the long queues of less favoured subjects waiting to share the experience. In December that same year, Lady Baillie listened to Edward VIII's abdication broadcast on a radio borrowed from one of her maids. She did not have one of her own.

Staff members were always assured of support and even maintenance in retirement. Several became members of a kind of extended family unit. Madame Fregosi, for instance, had been secretary to Lady Baillie's mother in New York but had left to marry, returning after her husband died to become a secretary to Dorothy Paget. When she retired, she was provided with accommodation in a flat at the castle until she was taken into care shortly before she died.

Another was Madame Southiere, who was the young Paget sisters' governess and who became governess to Lady Baillie's daughters, too, and lived in the castle as one of the family.

A number of employees remained at the castle for many years, including Stan Love and his wife, who were in charge of the laundry until Mrs Love died, after which the job was continued by George Martin. But one man in particular became the very backbone of all the restoration and maintenance work on the castle buildings virtually throughout his life. He was Joe Cooper, who first came to Leeds in 1911, when his father was the castle's estate foreman-carpenter.

After First World War service with the Royal Flying Corps, Joe joined the permanent staff at the castle and so was already in place when the new owners arrived in 1926. He remained to become foreman of the maintenance staff, house carpenter, and indispensible right-hand man and loyal friend of Lady Baillie.

As well as at Leeds, Joe carried out work at Harbourside, Lady Baillie's post-war home in the Bahamas, and became as familiar a figure there as he was in Kent. He outlived two wives and finally died, aged 88, in 1986.

Another staff stalwart was George Howard, who came to Leeds Castle with its new owners in 1926. Before they came to Leeds, the Wilson Filmers rented Bawdsey Manor near Felixstowe in Suffolk, the home of Sir Cuthbert and Lady Quilter from 1919-26. Olive Wilson Filmer was so impressed with the gardens there that when she bought Leeds Castle she persuaded the Quilters' head gardener, George Howard, to come to Kent with her and create the kind of gardens she wanted there.

He agreed and brought his family to live in a house that was enlarged and modernised for them in the right hand corner of the stable yard. He remained head gardener at Leeds until he retired and, in fact, died in the same year as Lady Baillie herself, 1974.

The reputation of the castle as a resort of so many famous film stars spread and attracted applications for domestic employment from girls with ambitions to become stars themselves. Some of the applications came from foreign girls, and after the war, particularly, several Scandinavian maids were employed. They hoped to attract the attention of guests who could further their ambitions and although some, at least, may well have attracted the attention they hoped for, there is no evidence that any of them achieved stardom as a result.

Although Lady Baillie could be a demanding employer, she was almost universally respected and liked by those who worked for her, most of whom regarded themselves very much as part of an exclusive community that made them, in a subtle but well-understood way, "superior" to other less favoured contemporaries.

Chapter Seven

THE GROUNDS AND THE ESTATE

During its long history, both the castle and the grounds have been changed a number of times by different owners and while the main reconstruction of the castle itself was going on throughout the last years of the Twenties, with further work after that, the restoration and creation of the gardens also went ahead.

George Howard faced a daunting task when he arrived at Leeds from Bawdsey to take over as head gardener. The whole place looked neglected and the first need was to recruit a corps of men to fell trees, dismantle collapsing out-buildings and lay out the paths and roadways that would form the skeleton of work that would follow. Everywhere was over-run by rats and rabbits which had to be got rid of before much else could be done.

He and Bill Watson came to Leeds in 1926 and were responsible for the new greenhouses which were actually built by James Gray (Chelsea) Horticultural Builders of Victoria Street, South-west London in 1927. George Howard created the wood garden, designed by the international garden designer, Russell Page, on what was formerly swampy ground watered by the River Len. Many thousands of spring bulbs were planted to create a breathtaking scene which became one of Lady Baillie's favourite places. Two small lakes were created, fed by the River Len, with small cascades to provide that specially delightful sound of moving water. A large number of rhododendrons and azaleas were planted near where clay tennis courts, built on the site of the Edward III mill, were provided with a heather thatched pavilion. This still has the oak balustrading that came from the castle's oak staircase, which was replaced by the wide stone one in the late 1920s. The tennis courts are no longer there but the pavilion survives, although its thatch has been replaced with tiles.

In the Thirties there were about twenty gardeners and, after the war, ten or eleven, including the dedicated greenhouse staff.

During Lady Baillie's time, the gardens not only supplied both the castle and the London house with fresh fruit, including peaches, grapes and the melons for which Leeds became famous, as well as vegetables, and flowers for the indoor arrangements, but they also sent produce for sale at Covent Garden market. Other produce for home consumption was provided by Park Barn Farm, the estate's home farm.

On one occasion, Lady Baillie acquired some seeds that had been taken from an excavated Egyptian tomb, which George propagated for her. They grew into corn – from seed that must have been at least two thousand years old.

In the largely derelict farmyard, most of the old weatherboarded buildings were demolished and the area cleared completely of the accumulated rubbish of many years. The 17th century barn (now the Fairfax Hall) was re-roofed and restored and a stable block for about thirty horses was built around the south and east of the barn. Two sides of a square to its north and east were taken up by new garages and parking spaces connected to the stable yard by an archway which had rooms above it for unmarried male staff and also for chauffeurs and other employees of visiting guests.

A large building known as The Bothy was built on the stable yard side of the garage yard to house single men and more employees' cottages were also provided.

Behind the garages, a laundry was built to deal with all the washing both for the castle and for the owners' London home as well. At the time it was built, it was one of the most modern private laundries in the country, equipped for a rapid turnover of very expensive, perfectly smooth, creaseless table and bed linen that could not have long survived commercial laundering.

We have Joe Cooper to thank for his account of how the water from eight springs in a field south of the Great Water was run into a well where a stone building housed a pump which filled a reservoir tank built on a high point south of the castle, beyond Park Barn Farm, large enough to hold 31,300 gallons of water. From there, the water was gravity-fed to a tank in one of the castle towers.

Immediately to the left of the inside of the gatehouse a coach house was converted into a squash court, lined with plaster of Paris and provided with a gallery. It is now the Dog Collar Museum.

The passage of heavy contractors' lorries during reconstruction work to the building itself caused the collapse of the old drive-way which ran straight from the gatehouse to a turning area in front of the castle entrance, and the top of a brick chamber was disclosed. There are traditions of other underground rooms, too, but before they could be professionally excavated, the driveways and paths were all relaid and the rooms remain one of the mysteries of the castle.

Towards the end of the Thirties, the large outdoor heated swimming pool, the first of its kind in England, was built alongside the Maiden's Tower, from where moat water was pumped and filtered. Before the pool was built, the children swam in the moat, which was both very cold and pretty filthy – but, of course, irresistible to youngsters.

Russell Page first came to Leeds in the late Thirties: a tall, dark, sharp-featured man. He already had many very wealthy clients in Europe and America and he became a valued friend and adviser to Lady Baillie. When, after the war, she embarked upon the Broomfield improvement programme, he was consulted about the cottage gardens, too.

Sir Adrian Baillie, himself an enthusiastic and very able golfer, had a nine-hole golf course laid out at Leeds in 1931-2 by Sir Guy Campbell, who designed a similar one in America. It became acknowledged as the best of its kind in this country and was a favourite of many of the world's top players. Lady Baillie was not a golfer and her main interest in the golf course was that it should not detract from the castle's setting. She insisted that no bunker should be visible from the castle and no flag on the greens should break the skyline. The result, of course, was an immaculately landscaped sward sweeping down to the very edge of the moat, adding materially to the attractiveness of the castle itself.

Sir Adrian also created the estate's shooting drives during the

1930s. The estate included about 750 acres of woodland but in the early 1930s efforts were made to improve the shooting and a series of fir plantations were added: Ashen Wood, Hawk Wood, Church Wood and Leeds Covert. On average, about 3,000 pheasants were reared on the estate every year, about half of which were shot.

Shooting was another outdoor pursuit that did not find particular favour with Lady Baillie, although she recognised it was an inevitable feature of country life. It is on record, however, that she expressed her displeasure in no uncertain terms when some of her ornamental pheasants were accidentally shot during one of the drives. The gun responsible never came to Leeds again.

Later, in the mid-1950s, as part of an overall programme of renovation of the entire estate, a scheme of regeneration was agreed with the Forestry Commission, and some areas of the woods were replanted with nearly three-quarters of a million trees over a five-year period, from the southern boundaries of Abbey and Kings Woods to the top of the Downs above Greenway Court. An entirely new woodland area was created on Broomfield Bank, adjacent to Park Barn Farm, down towards the River Len.

Chapter Eight

THE COLLECTIONS

Although Lady Baillie went to considerable lengths, sometimes, to acquire items that she believed would be right for Leeds Castle, she was not a collector in the sense that some are. She did not, for example, set out to collect all the examples of any particular artist's work, or of any particular style or period of furniture or porcelain.

Her acquisitiveness was directed towards buying pieces that would complement the particular décor she and, of course, Armand-Albert Rateau and Stéphane Boudin were aiming to achieve at any one time. She became well known to dealers throughout Europe as a keenly competitive buyer and she learned to bargain with the best of them, but she was less concerned with the value of her purchases than with their appropriateness. Equally, if something took her fancy she would buy it, if she could, and decide where was the perfect place for it afterwards. Whatever she bought, and whatever it cost, she derived great pleasure from her acquisitions and kept typically meticulous records of all her purchases.

Although she collected paintings and tapestries, porcelain and clocks, glassware and carpets – and even exotic birds and waterfowl – it was the furniture with which she complemented the castle interior that perhaps best illustrated the taste and discernment that Lady Baillie, later advised and guided by Stéphane Boudin, contributed to the castle during her time there. Much of it has since been sold, but enough remains to illustrate the effect she strove to achieve.

This is not the place to recite a full or even an abridged inventory of her many acquisitions. They included some very fine Louis XIV, XV and XVI cabinet work but not all the pieces were of French origin or inspiration. Her 18th century English and 17th century Spanish four-poster beds are still in use in the castle today, and her collection included 17th and 18th century Italian tables, an early 19th century Sino-Dutch tallboy and Victorian papier-mâché chairs.

Nor was everything necessarily old; in particular, commodes in two of the bedrooms at Leeds were designed by Boudin in the 1930s. The most important aim was that a piece should look right in its new surroundings.

Nevertheless, much of what she bought to furnish the castle was old. Items included 18th century English and Russian carpets, 18th century German and Italian toilet sets, 18th century Venetian blackamoor figures and 19th century candelabra.

With few exceptions, the emphasis of the pieces that Lady Baillie collected was on the decorative or, at the least, the eye-catching rather than the purely utilitarian. She liked pretty things, which might explain why, although she collected a number of interesting clocks, they did not include a single long-case (grandfather) clock.

Her collection, however, included a great many paintings, of which a number were Flemish portraits of children, in which she took particular delight. Several fine Old Masters were represented, including Giambattista Tiepolo the elder (1696-1770), whose picture *The Pulchinello's Kitchen* is still to be seen at the castle, in the Yellow Drawing Room.

Many of the pictures hint at the private person behind the public reserve of the woman who owned them. Her boudoir, for instance, had a rather charming picture of a young woman watching in a mirror as her hair is being dressed. It was exhibited in Paris in 1959 with the title *La Toilette* and in New York in 1979 as *Devant La Glace*. It was painted by Eva Gonzalez (1849-83), who also painted *Le Départ*, a somewhat poignant picture of a lady standing beside a suitcase, which is still at Leeds Castle, hanging in the Seminar Room.

Lady Baillie took particular delight, too, in pictures of birds and flowers, and studies of songbirds by Christoph Ludwig Agricola (1677-1719) complement still life paintings of summer flowers by Louis Vidal (c 1754), Pierre-Joseph Redouté (1759-1840), and others. During the 1970s, Philip Rickman (1891-

1982) was a particular favourite of hers and he painted a series of watercolours of birds, many in her aviary, which now hang in the Boardroom corridor.

Some of her collection of French impressionist and post-impressionist paintings can still be seen at Leeds, although a double-sided cartoon by Henri Toulouse-Lautrec (1864-1901) is no longer among them. Two artists who became favourites of Lady Baillie in later life were Maurice Brianchon (1899-1979) and André Dunoyer de Segonzac (1884-1974), whose paintings hang in the Seminar Room.

Several portaits of members of her family remain at the castle, including those of her parents, Lord Queenborough, by Arthur Hacker (1858-1919), and her mother, formerly Miss Pauline Whitney, by Howard Cushing (1869-1916), and also of her ancestors Lord Alfred and Lord George Paget by John James Chalon (1778-1854).

One of the few publicly displayed representations of Lady Baillie herself is that in which she sits against a table, with her two daughters, Pauline and Susan, in the Thorpe Hall Room at Leeds Castle. It was painted by Etienne Drian (1885-1961), who also drew two amusing pictures, both entitled *The Duet*, which hang in her bedroom. One shows two monkeys in evening dress, one playing a banjo and the other a violin. The other picture is also of two monkeys (the same two?), one of them singing while the other plays a banjo. The often-mentioned reserve that Lady Baillie exhibited in public could give the impression that she lacked a very lively sense of humour. Pictures such as these belie that, as does another gently risqué picture of a Lady Godiva-like woman riding a horse as she reviews a parade of guardsmen. This hangs in one of her private bedrooms.

As well as paintings, Lady Baillie bought a number of tapestries. Some of them remain, including a rare Enghien armorial tapestry in the Banqueting Hall, two Flemish mid-sixteeenth century *feuilles de choux* tapestries in the inner hall, and five Louis XVI Aubusson or Beauvais pastoral tapestry panels in the dining room.

Visitors to the castle can still see some of the porcelain that made up an important part of Lady Baillie's collection. In the dining room, for example, there are displays of Chinese porcelain, as arranged by Stéphane Boudin, and there is more in the Yellow Drawing Room and the Thorpe Hall Room. They include beautifully decorated dishes, tureens with covers and stands, vases, jars and figures of birds.

The porcelain collection also included some particularly fine pieces of Meissen birds and animals, as well as examples of German, English and Italian work of different periods.

Although many of her acquisitions were bought with Leeds in mind, others were destined for her London home and many were treated as interchangeable. An item might be bought for Leeds, where it would stay for a while and then be taken to London, or vice versa, or even disposed of if it did not fit in with a changed décor in order for a more appropriate piece to be bought instead.

Her penchant for collecting was not confined to furniture and other works of art. During the last twenty years of her life, particularly, her collection of exotic birds became something of a passion. There were birds at Leeds before the Second World War, including a toucan, a macaw and various parrots, as well as the black swans and flamingoes on the moat. But in the early 1950s, Lady Baillie broke her leg during a winter stay in the Bahamas and to relieve the tedium of inactivity necessitated by the prescribed rest, she decided to develop her life-long interest in birds.

The black swans that had graced the moat pre-war had had to be evacuated during the war and never returned, but after the war they were replaced with a pair given to her by her cousin, Whitney Straight.

As always, Lady Baillie sought expert advice, in this case from the Keston Foreign Bird Park at Bromley, which, at the time, was the only such bird park in the world. As a result, two small aviaries were built on the terrace near the swimming pool, where Lady Baillie could lie in a long chair and watch the four varieties of Australian finches that were housed in them. Breeding increased the number of birds and, once she was able to walk again, she began to visit the Keston bird park and to introduce other exotic specimens to Leeds.

Before long, inevitably, larger accommodation was needed, and two more aviaries, with pineapple finials, were built on Stable Hill, looking out across the Len valley. The siting was Boudin's idea, intended to ensure that no view of the castle was marred by anything as aesthetically dubious as outsize bird cages.

A young under-gardener called Peter Taylor volunteered to become the keeper of the birds and he and Lady Baillie became close friends, united by their interest in birds, which developed into an ambition to build up the most complete collection of Australian parakeets in Europe. More aviaries were built until, when she died in 1974, there were 120, plus four indoor bird rooms, being looked after by four full-time keepers.

Lady Baillie made several expeditions to various parts of Europe to see some of the great collections of exotic birds, in Germany, Holland and Belgium particularly, and one of these has been amusingly recalled by her former agent, John Money. It took the two of them to a converted mill in Haan, near Dusseldorf, where a father and two brothers had what Mr Money described as "an Aladdin's cave of birds".

It was during that post-war period when there were restrictions on how much money English people could spend abroad and Mr Money found himself worrying that Lady Baillie's enthusiasm was overtaking her spending power. However, when the time came to settle the bill, she had one look at the total cost and took out from her handbag a red crayon with which she drew a line through the figure. She halved it, wrote in the new figure and declared with characteristic finality: "I pay this."

After some debate, the figure was agreed. It was still a considerable sum and when Mr Money presented a Bank of England draft to be cashed at the local bank, it caused some consternation. The bank was cleared of other customers, doors closed and locked and bank clerks sent hurrying off to collect sufficient ready cash from neighbouring shops and other places to meet the need.

The transaction completed at last, the newly-purchased birds were borne off to the airport where they prompted a new furore, this time among officials and Customs men. Because they had not known what they were going to buy, the English bird-fanciers had no appropriate papers. They were told the birds must travel as freight, but that was not something Lady Baillie could accept. A telephone call was made to the headquarters of the British Overseas Airways Corporation in England (of which, fortunately, Lady Baillie's cousin, Whitney Straight, happened to be chairman – a particularly apposite illustration of the advantage of having friends in high places), and the English pair were accommodated in a part of the aircraft from which the front row of seats had been removed specially so that the boxes containing the birds could travel with them, at their feet.

The story ended with their arrival back at Lady Baillie's London house, where Peter Taylor was waiting to whisk the birds off to their new home at Leeds. Although the travellers had been up since very early that morning, Lady Baillie proposed an immediate celebratory dinner and a visit to a cinema, from which Mr Money eventually arrived home, exhausted by the day's events, at about one o'clock next morning.

In the 1960s, she made one trip even farther afield, to Swaziland in Southern Africa and on to Madagascar and Australia where she met Sir Edward Halstrom, owner of the greatest collection of Australian parakeets, cockatoos and other birds ever put together. He offered the entire collection to Lady Baillie, together with an endowment for its maintenance in England after he died, but the Australian government refused to permit it and all she actually brought back from "Down Under" were three more black swans.

Not all the acquisitions were made abroad, however. Mr Money has also recalled occasions when they were chauffeur-driven into the East End of London to conduct business in some back-garden aviary where a particular bird had been brought to her attention.

"She was a great believer in cash," Mr Money reminisced. "I

often found myself handed a brown tradesman's envelope into which was stuffed a quite considerable sum and it was my job to pay out when the time came."

Such forays were likely to provoke a great deal of interest from the neighbourhood children, with whom Lady Baillie usually found a few moments for an exchange of pleasantries before she returned to her car, which itself was always the object of great local curiosity.

Lady Baillie was a Fellow of the Zoological Society and visited the London Zoo to seek veterinary advice from time to time as well as to see the animals. She even, on at least two occasions, went into the enclosures, once with a snow leopard and, another time, with the original giant panda.

The Leeds Castle collection of Australian parakeets gained an international reputation. They were one of the features that HM the Queen Mother particularly asked to see when she visited the castle while she was staying with Peter Cazalet, who trained her racehorses, at Fairlawne, near Tonbridge.

It was not only cage birds that interested Lady Baillie. The purchase of various ornamental ducks from a lady in Wiltshire led to the establishment of The Duckery. This was completely redesigned by Russell Page and stocked with the same acquisitive zeal as the aviaries, this time with the head gamekeeper George Riggall taking on the role of duck keeper.

Eventually, there were some thirty different varieties of duck, which shared life in the castle grounds with the peacocks, the ornamental pheasants and the black swans.

What became known as the *Pavilion de Canard* was built by Ted Filmer, the stone mason, for Lady Baillie to sit in and watch the ducks, and in the last two years of her life her birds were one of her major interests. Even after she was confined to a wheelchair and needed a constantly available supply of oxygen she still took an active and almost daily interest in their welfare.

Chapter Nine

THE WAR YEARS

When the war started in September 1939, few Britons doubted that Germany and the Nazis would quickly be taught the error of their ways and there was a confident expectation that it would all be over by Christmas.

Life at Leeds Castle went on much as it had done throughout the decade. The windows had to be blacked out, of course, and the family cars' lights dimmed. Food rationing was not introduced until the beginning of 1940 but by that time the optimism about an early end to the war was already fading.

In his autobiography, *The Moon's A Balloon*, the actor David Niven wrote of his visit to the castle in 1940: "The last weekend before I went to Tidworth [to join the Army] I was invited to the home of Sir Adrian and Lady Baillie, Leeds Castle, where I was to see some of the big wheels of government at play."

The "big wheels of government" sharing that weekend with him at Leeds included David Margesson, Government Chief Whip and soon to become Secretary of State for War in Churchill's coalition government; Geoffrey Lloyd, then Secretary for Mines; and Harcourt ("Crinks") Johnstone, the Liberal Whip who died in 1945.

Niven wrote: "As a group they depressed me. I had the feeling that they had no right to eat and drink and dress for dinner, make small talk and gossip like ordinary people. I was quite unreasonably shocked that they were not locked in their offices for the weekend, working tirelessly to find ways to finish the war before it got properly started."

David Margesson and Geoffrey Lloyd, who were widely regarded as among the best-informed members of the government, would have been aware of the inevitability of war for some time. Geoffry Lloyd had been given full-time responsibility for air raid precautions when he was Parliamentary Under-Secretary at the Home Office in June 1938.

Before war was declared, arrangements were made for the Baillie heir, five year old Gawaine, to go to family friends in America, where he remained for the duration.

At the same time, Lady Baillie offered to send children of estate staff on a six months' "holiday" to America. Only three parents agreed to let their children go but one of those was unable to do so, on her doctor's advice. The other two went and stayed there for six years. Both returned to Leeds when the war was over, one to a mother whose husband had been killed in a tractor accident while he was tending the castle golf course.

The almost complacent optimism of the "phoney war" period was rudely shattered in the spring of 1940 when the German blitzkrieg swept through the Netherlands, Belgium and Northern France and forced the Dunkirk evacuation upon the British Expeditionary Force. Suddenly, the war became very near and nowhere in Britain more than in the south-eastern corner and in Kent in particular.

Entertaining at Leeds Castle on the pre-war scale ended abruptly. The war reduced castle staff from a pre war forty-six to nine as men and women were called up to the Services or other war work and the castle found itself with new roles.

At the outbreak of the war, it was decided that the British Red Cross Society and St John Joint War Organisation should be responsible for the administration and staffing of suitable country houses throughout Britain that were capable of providing between fifty and a hundred beds to treat wounded servicemen and women. The original intention was that the War Office would requisition such houses and then hand them over to the Organisation for alteration, adaptation and administration. In fact, no formal requisitions were needed and the Organisation took over all the properties under private agreements with their owners.

Leeds Castle was one of these. Lady Baillie inherited an interest in nursing from her American grandfather, William Whitney, who made substantial endowments to medical research establishments in America, and from her mother and father.

When Almeric Paget brought his wife, Pauline, to England from America, they settled in Suffolk, where Almeric became High Sheriff in 1909. Mrs Paget was a generous patron of Addenbrooke's Hospital and she also gave financial help to many other organisations.

At the outbreak of World War I, Mr and Mrs Paget offered the War Office the free services of a Massage Corps of fifty masseurs for war-wounded men. Later, when the demand increased, the number of masseurs was increased to 130, still maintained at the expense of the Pagets until the War Office took over responsibility for providing masseurs for the entire army and a camp was opened at Eastbourne. The Pagets were asked to organise the camp and to provide the women to staff it with the help of a government grant.

Subsequently more camps were opened and military hospitals turned to the Almeric Paget Massage Corps which, by the summer of 1916, was 1,086 strong, with its headquarters at 39 Berkeley Square in London. The Pagets also financed free out-patient treatment for officers and men at 55 Portland Place, London and Mrs Paget established a 20-bed convalescent hospital where no expense was spared on the treatment and comfort of her patients.

When Mrs Paget died from heart failure in November 1916 her funeral was attended by wounded soldiers from the Eastbourne camp and some of them carried her coffin to its burial at St Mary's Church at Hertingfordbury.

Mr Paget earned a knighthood for his public and charitable services and later became Lord Queenborough. He died, aged 88, in September 1949.

Lady Baillie herself served with the Red Cross as a VAD (Voluntary Aid Detachment) nurse in 1918 and when Leeds Castle became a hospital in 1940 she once again donned uniform although it was not, in fact, a regular Red Cross officer's uniform and her position was a purely honorary one.

When the first VADs arrived, in June 1940, just after the Dunkirk evacuation, the Leeds Castle hospital had no patients and the young nurses set about making themselves at home. Lady Baillie assumed there were patients in the beds and brought some weekend guests to visit them. Finding only the nurses, she immediately set about re-housing them and for the rest of their time at Leeds they were quartered in the stable yard, where they occupied the archway rooms formerly used by unmarried men on the castle staff.

In July 1940, the castle was occupied by 10 Coy, Royal Army Medical Corps and throughout the Battle of Britain, in August and September, 1940, the hospital treated casualties from the air war, friend and foe alike. Some of the airmen arrived still harnessed to the parachutes that had saved their lives. An operating theatre was set up in what is now the Green Bedroom on the first floor of the main building and one of the first casualties to be treated there was a German pilot who had parachuted out of his plane and had to have a leg amputated.

The Commandant of the VADs at Leeds was Lady Winefride Howard, sister of the Duke of Norfolk, who had her administrative centre in the Maiden's Tower. The Baillie family moved into the gloriette, where they continued to live for most of the duration of the war. Lady Baillie's younger daughter, Susan, was seventeen and she decided she was quite old enough to follow in her mother's footsteps and become a VAD nurse and work in the castle hospital wards, which she did.

The young nurses who were posted to Leeds worked under the supervision and direction of a matron, nursing sisters and staff nurses of the Queen Alexandra's Imperial Military Nursing Service, and some of their memories of nursing at Leeds Castle were included in a book called *Once Upon A Ward* which was published by Doreen Boys in 1980.

One recalled accepting a lift into Maidstone in a car driven by a man wearing the uniform of an Air Raid Precaution (ARP) Warden which, however, proved to be covering the field grey of the German pilot who had stolen the disguise. He had been shot down and was trying to reach the coast. When the car ran out of petrol, he drew a revolver which he pointed at the bewildered nurse, indicating in more eloquent gestures than his limited English allowed that she should stay in the car while he made off into nearby woods. Unfortunately for him, he was heading in the wrong direction and was caught about an hour later.

In spite of the constant aerial warfare overhead, most of the nurses were well pleased with their posting to Leeds. It was a beautiful place in which to work, with the ancient stonework reflected in the quiet water of the moat, on which glided both black and white swans, while llamas and other exotic animals roamed the grounds. The girls could use the superb golf course and the swimming pool beside the Maiden's Tower, which was one of the finest private pools in the country.

While some were accommodated in the castle's stable yard, others were billetted with local families and an office was set up for the medical staff in one of the looseboxes formerly occupied by Dorothy Paget's race horses.

Best of all, though, because they were, after all, still young women under the uniforms they wore to work, the whole Kentish countryside was crammed with servicemen, especially after Dunkirk. When New Zealand troops camped at nearby Hollingbourne the nurses were never short of invitations to dances and parties organised by them. There was an officers' club in one of the hotels near Maidstone East railway station, to which they were sometimes invited and dances were held at the Star Hotel (now remembered only by the Star Arcade in the High Street).

When Lady Baillie's elder daughter, Pauline, was married in 1940, the nurses were all invited to the reception.

Relations between the medical staff and the domestic staff at the hospital were not always entirely harmonious. The well-known problems that can arise when too many cooks share the same kitchen caused some friction with the Baillies' French chef, who grudgingly permitted his equipment to be used but only when he did not need it in order to prepare food for his employers. When he did, one of the hospital cooks recalled, he was apt simply to remove anything that was being cooked by anyone else to make way for his own needs.

Once the Battle of Britain was won, the hospital was emptied of patients. Leeds is not much more than about 20 miles from the Channel coast and, with the threat of imminent invasion, it was judged unsafe. The VADs were transferred to the military hospital that was set up in the grounds of what was then Barming Mental Hospital, on the Tonbridge side of Maidstone, where some of them remained until 1943. Then, many of them resigned and took up alternative war work elsewhere rather than be taken over by the Army and have to submit to Army regulations and possible postings overseas.

Only after the threat of invasion receded was Leeds Castle re-opened, this time as a hospital for officers only.

After the Dunkirk evacuation, General Thorne, who commanded 12 Corps, which was responsible for the defence of Kent and Sussex, met David Margesson at Leeds where, together, they made plans to meet the expected German invasion. Later on, General Bernard Montgomery (who had not yet earned the popular nickname of *Monty* which followed the success of his North African campaign) also met the Defence Secretary at Leeds.

One of the men who visited the castle during that fraught year of 1940 was Admiral Sir Bertram Ramsay, who masterminded the Dunkirk evacuation from his headquarters in Dover Castle and who was later Commander-in-Chief, Allied Navies, for the D-day invasion of Europe in June 1944. It was the Admiral's concerns for the defence of the Channel ports that led to the highly secret experiments carried out under the direction of Geoffrey Lloyd who, in 1940, was the Minister in charge of the secret Petroleum Warfare Department. At that time, Britain was poorly armed to repel an invasion of any strength at all and there were no anti-tank guns between London and the coast. With the help of some brilliant oil industry engineers, a system was devised that would enable beaches and even the sea itself to be set on fire, which invading troops would have to penetrate before they could land.

After the invasion threat was past, the department went from the defensive to the offensive and developed the *Churchill Crocodile* flame-throwing tank, which proved to be very successful in action. Some of these top secret experiments were carried out on the open spaces of the Leeds Castle golf course where any accidents were unlikely to be too serious, and although some of them scorched the grass very badly, that was one of the sacrifices the castle and its owners made for the war effort.

After the castle was no longer a hospital, in 1943, some of the "guinea pigs" of Sir Archibald McIndoe's pioneering plastic surgery at the Queen Victoria Hospital at East Grinstead were invited to Leeds Castle to convalesce. One of those was Paul Hart, a founder-member of the *Guinea Pig Club*, who returned to the castle several times during 1943 and 1944 for stays of two or three weeks at a time as the guest of Lady Baillie. Fifty years later, he still remembered her as a very beautiful and very charming lady.

"She was not there during the week, but we had the run of the house and at weekends she came with other guests, including some of the leading war-time figures," he recalled.

The men of the castle staff who remained at home joined the Local Defence Volunteers, later to be called the Home Guard. They came under the command of Brigadier-General H Franklin, who was Zone Commander of the LDV in Kent. In May 1940 he asked Col W Baker to form a local defence force to which 200 rifles were allocated and some of these were stored at Leeds Castle. The rest were kept at Maidstone Police Station.

There were, in fact, eight volunteers for the first Maidstone local defence force, known as Parashots because it was supposed that the greatest immediate threat would come from German paratroops whom the local men would have to shoot as they floated to earth. In the absence of uniforms of any kind, the volunteers were identified only by the white handkerchief each man tied round his upper arm and it was not until later that year that the name "Home Guard" came into use, after the Prime Minister, Winston Churchill, used the phrase in a speech, and proper military uniforms began to be issued.

Within a week of the first call, however, there were 1,000 volunteers in Kent and the Maidstone area, including Leeds, which had more than 400 of them. Leeds had its own section of the Hollingbourne platoon with a command post at Abbey Farm in Leeds village. They were called to a number of incidents, mostly involving crashed aeroplanes, but the nearest they came to anything like earnest action was when a German airman parachuted safely onto the castle golf course. He was seen descending and the Hollingbourne platoon Home Guard commander was alerted. A day-long search followed, during which a Home Guard on duty on a wooden bridge across Broomfield Road saw the fugitive and held him at rifle-point.

Unfortunately the German was on the road below the bridge and his captor could not go down and take him prisoner without giving him the opportunity to make a run for it. So the two men stayed where they were, one at each end of a levelled rifle, until the platoon commander turned up and was able to take charge of the prisoner, who by that time was probably only too happy to go quietly.

Lady Baillie herself lived much of the time in London, where she carried out voluntary work for a Services club, travelling down to Leeds at weekends whenever she could.

The castle itself survived the war without damage, despite the bombs that dropped in the grounds and killed one of the llamas. According to official Kent County Council figures released after the war, 946 high explosive bombs, 19 oil bombs, two land mines and 1,720 incendiary bombs were dropped on the Hollingbourne rural district, which included the castle and its grounds. Twenty-one enemy aeroplanes also crashed into the district. The parishes of Leeds, Otham and Langley, however, formed a little island in the middle of Kent that remained entirely free from the county-wide infestation of "doodlebugs" (as the V1 flying bombs were called), although the rest of the rural district was hit by 81 of them altogether and two of those fell in Broomfield, part of the Leeds Castle estate.

Ten people were killed by war action in the district and

another 58 were injured, but only the relatively small number of 11 properties were totally destroyed, although 1,706 were damaged.

During the the war, a tented camp was set up in the castle park. After a while, the tents were replaced with Nissen huts, but they were only occupied for a short time and when the war was over they were cleared away with the help of German and Italian prisoners of war waiting to be repatriated.

Throughout the war, the castle remained a haven for government ministers and other guests. Sir Henry "Chips" Channon, the Chicago-born American and life-long Anglophile, who became a naturalised Englishman and was a Member of Parliament for more than twenty years, recorded in his diaries on August 9, 1942: "Leeds Castle, chez Olive Baillie. Only the flapping of the swans on the moat disturbed me and I slept eleven hours and woke like a pygmy refreshed. We sunbathed, over-ate, drank champagne, gossipped all day. I was gay and amusing and for once forgot the war and our anxieties. "

Again, in April 1943, he was at Leeds during one very warm weekend. He noted: "It was a lyrical day – the heat, the gauze-like mist rising from the fruit blossoms, the spinach-green fields – all were intoxicating, as was the grey castle rising from the moat as I approached it. Black swans followed by cygnets were swimming around. "

The next day (April 18) was "the hottest day I can ever remember in England". He spent it lying "almost naked until 7. 30pm, wearing only slacks for luncheon, when I revelled in plovers' eggs and champagne".

Wartime hardship seems to have been a relative term at Leeds. Lady Baillie's long-time very close friendship with Geoffrey Lloyd, who was Parliamentary Secretary (Petroleum) at the Board of Trade from 1940 to 1942, and Parliamentary Secretary for Petroleum, Ministry of Fuel and Power, from 1942 until 1945, led envious people to assert that she did not suffer as acutely as less-favoured contemporaries from petrol shortages but, of course, there is no actual evidence of that. Lady Baillie's personal war effort remains, like so much of the personal life she guarded so closely, almost entirely unrecorded. Her husband, Sir Adrian, served the country with similarly little impact on recorded history, although staff at the castle understood that his work "*had something to do with the Free French Forces*".

During the war, of course, there was a general acceptance that no-one talked about their work because, as the posters constantly reminded everyone, "*Careless Talk Costs Lives*". It would have been an unnecessary reminder to Lady Baillie, whose natural lifelong discretion made it a slogan with which she could sympathise wholeheartedly.

Chapter Ten

THE END OF AN ERA

After the war ended in 1945, there was no going back to pre-war life as though nothing had happened. Too much had happened for that to be possible.

Britain was plunged into austerity on a scale that surpassed even war-time restrictions. As the country huddled around inadequate fuel supplies through the coldest winter anyone could remember, rationing not only continued but, in some respects, became even more strict. An election shock swept Clement Attlee's Labour government into a frenzy of nationalisation and enervating austerity.

At Leeds Castle, Lady Baillie settled to a quieter life with her family and became more the country landowner than the glittering hostess. Although there were weekend parties again, usually about three or four a year, they were not the same. Everyone was older for one thing, and guests now included sons and daughters of pre-war party-goers. There was still sometimes dancing in the saloon, with backgammon, bridge and canasta as alternative evening entertainments.

But Lady Baillie's health was not robust and, more and more, she turned her thoughts and energies to her role of custodian of one of the gems of Kentish heritage and to making sure she bequeathed it to a posterity that could value and enjoy it.

The family moved back into the main castle building where life went on at a rather gentler pace. The gloriette became a store for various pieces from the collections and was used once a year for the children's Christmas parties that were resumed.

Later, the gloriette was the venue for the great party that Sir Gawaine gave for the castle staff and tenants soon after his marriage in 1966 to his Canadian bride, Margot Gardner.

Lady Baillie's elder daughter, Pauline, had married in 1940 Group Captain the Hon Edward Ward, RAF, but the marriage was dissolved in 1947. She married three times more, in 1948, 1960 and 1974, dying in 1984 as Mrs Edward Lee Cave.

The other daughter, Susan, was 22 when the war ended and a year later she married Captain the Hon Geoffrey Russell, who later became 4th Baron Ampthill. In 1972, she married again, this time Colonel Edward Remington-Hobbs, who died in 1998. She continued to live in the Maiden's Tower at the castle until she died in 2001.

After a distinguished career in the House of Commons, during which he was briefly, in 1942, in the running for the Conservative party leadership, David Margesson was raised to the peerage as the first Viscount Margesson and for the next 20 years subsided into relative obscurity as a member of the House of Lords. He continued to figure in life at Leeds, however, where he was generally regarded as a genial and unfailingly courteous man and he became Lady Baillie's principal adviser about the estate generally.

Geoffrey Lloyd, too, having held important governmental posts throughout the war, became Minister of Information in 1945, Minister of Fuel and Power from 1951 to 1955 and Minister of Education from 1957 to 1959. He assumed the title of Baron Geoffrey-Lloyd of Broomfield when he was created a life peer in 1974.

The castle continued to open its grounds to the public from time to time in order to raise funds for various organisations. It had always been a popular venue and when, in July 1949, a fete was held for the benefit of the Maidstone Divisional Conservative Association, with a dog show, various stalls, competitions and other attractions, it was estimated that nearly 4,000 people came through the turnstiles during the day. The fete was opened by Alfred Bossom, Maidstone's Conservative MP, and it ended with dancing on the green.

The castle still numbered royalty among its guests. Queen Elizabeth, the Queen Mother, came several times, as did Princess Marina, Duchess of Kent. Another fairly frequent visitor to the castle was Lady Baillie's cousin, the multi-millionaire John Hay Whitney, after he was appointed US Ambassador to Britain by

President Dwight Eisenhower. "Jock" Whitney, as he was known familiarly, had made extended visits to England before the war and had been in London in 1942 as a US Army captain. He was an enthusiastic golfer who enjoyed playing on the Leeds golf course.

Post-war Christmases at Leeds were mainly family affairs, with Lady Baillie, her three half-sisters, two daughters, their children and old family friends gathered in rooms decorated with huge swags of paper chains, just as they were in the "good old days" before the war. There were enormous arrangements of specially grown flowers from the castle greenhouses in all the rooms and a complete bough of mistletoe was always cut from a tree in the grounds.

Everyone staying at the castle for Christmas was expected to attend matins at Leeds church on Christmas morning, filling several of the front rows of pews. Lunch was a relaxed meal so that the staff could enjoy their Christmas dinner at midday and be ready for the main event of the day, the family dinner in the evening.

On Boxing Day it was traditional to hold a shoot specially for the younger members of the family who were considered old enough to use a gun under the supervision of some of the adults. For the rest, there was croquet, if the weather was fine, strolls through the grounds and visits to the aviaries and greenhouses.

A description of Christmas at Leeds Castle after the war was included in *A Kent Christmas* by G and F Doel but generally there was less entertaining now. There were fewer staff than there had been before the war and it was not unknown for guests to be invited to amuse themselves by helping to clear some of the brambles and nettles that threatened to overwhelm the rhododendrons in the wood garden.

Lady Baillie's love of flowers, in massed displays throughout the house, kept staff busy throughout Fridays preparing arrangements in readiness for her arrival for the weekend. Like everything else connected with the interior – and, in some cases, out of doors as well – the flowers had to conform to colour schemes and positions advised by Stéphane Boudin.

In 1950 Lady Baillie recruited a new resident agent in John Money, who remained in the post with her for twenty-five years. His involvement with the castle lasted for more than forty years and it is his reminiscences that have told us much of what we know about life at the castle during that period.

The 1950s began a major renaissance programme for the estate as a whole. The entire hamlet of Broomfield was reorganised, all seventeen cottages and three farmhouses were completely modernised, and bathrooms were installed.

In 1952, Lady Baillie's deteriorating health led her to acquire a property in the Bahamas called Harbourside and after that she spent most of the winter months there. Just before Christmas, the butler's wife, Mrs Borrett, normally went to the house on Hog Island (later renamed Paradise Island) to prepare for Lady Baillie's arrival early in the New Year. Then, accompanied by Mr Borrett and about eight other members of the Leeds staff, as well as her private secretary and her maid, Lady Baillie made the trip by one of the trans-Atlantic liners. She stayed abroad until March, in the relaxing warmth of Paradise Island, where house parties were virtually continuous, with much the same guests sharing the sunshine with her every year.

The house there was given the same kind of refurbishment that Leeds Castle had had when she first moved into it, with the help of the ever present Stéphane Boudin. Much of the decorative details, including the panels of sea-shells set into plaster of Paris that Boudin designed specially for her bedroom, were made in the Paris workshops of Maison Jansen and shipped out, to be reassembled in Nassau, often under the direction of Joe Cooper.

During the summer, in England, Lady Baillie could still dazzle guests with her talents as a hostess whenever she held a ball at her London home. One of these was recorded by Chips Channon in his diary for 13 July, 1950 when he described the garden, which was transformed by M Boudin into a ballroom edged with floodlit herbaceous borders. Princess Margaret was among the guests on that occasion and the diarist noted that she stayed until 4.30 am. He also recorded that Frank Sinatra, who was appearing at the London Palladium that year, crooned for half an hour – "to everyone's intense boredom".

It was while she was in the Bahamas that Lady Baillie suffered an accident that put her into hospital in Miami for three weeks. One stormy night she slipped on some highly polished Italian tiles outside the main entrance to the house and suffered a compound fracture of one of her legs. The weather made it impossible for a doctor to cross the mile of water from Nassau to the island and so the castle carpenter, who was with them, provided splints and Borrett was able to set the leg and get the patient indoors.

Thanks to the treatment she received, she regained full use of the leg, while the tiles were covered with rubber matting to prevent any further accidents of that kind.

It was that accident, and her need to find something to interest her while she recovered back at Leeds, that led to the development of her interest in exotic birds and the collection that became a feature of the castle grounds.

Lady Baillie's sister, Dorothy Paget, died in 1960 and although they had not shared the close relationship of their youth for many years, nevertheless it was a keenly felt loss. So was the loss, at Christmas 1965, of Lord Margesson who died at the house on Paradise Island.

Then, in 1967, her long and happy association with Stéphane Boudin ended with his death and although his nephew, Claude Mandron, who had worked with him, carried on his work at Leeds and elsewhere, it was yet another sad blow for Lady Baillie.

In the winter of 1972-3, with her health deteriorating rapidly, she insisted on making the customary journey to Harbourside and while she was there she collapsed one stormy evening on to the floor of her bedroom. The butler, Borrett, took charge of the situation. Called from his bed by a distraught maid, he found Lady Baillie in her room, apparently dead, but he was able to get her breathing again and then he telephoned a doctor on the mainland. Again, the weather made it impossible for the doctor to reach the island and so, with the help of an ex-naval footman, the unconscious woman was taken to a boat which made the crossing to the Royal Bank of Canada dock where an ambulance was waiting to rush her to the Princess Margaret Hospital. She recovered and returned to England but when, the following year, she prepared to make the journey to the Bahamas as usual, the Borretts said they would not go with her because they felt the responsibility would be too great. So, instead, that year she was accompanied by one of the castle footmen who suffered from epilepsy and, in fact, died there during that winter.

She was now a very sick woman, dependent upon oxygen to help her breathing and with a resident nurse, Al Murphy, always in attendance, although Lady Baillie made something of a game of trying to escape from her ministrations.

Geoffrey Lloyd remained a constant companion. He had a large yacht and was sometimes part of the Harbourside household for two months at a time. He was with her in the South of France during the last few weeks of her life. She actually died in London on 9 September, 1974, shortly after returning from France and without seeing her beloved Leeds Castle again.

The 3,400 acres of the Leeds Castle agricultural estate had been owned by Sir Gawaine Baillie since 1966 but for some time before her death Lady Baillie had been discussing with her advisers how best to achieve her wishes for the castle. She was very anxious that everything should be settled during her lifetime so that she could approve whatever arrangements were made.

She did not want the castle to become a National Trust property, but she knew that if she left it to any individual it would attract a crippling eighty per cent death duty. This would not have left enough money for its maintenance so that it would have had to be sold and perhaps become, at that time, a casino or exclusive country club of some kind. She did not want that, either. She wanted the castle to be available to the public as a unique centre for the arts and medical conferences. She had, of course, a family background of interest in medical matters which she shared with Geoffrey Lloyd, who had a great fund of medical knowledge and a considerable personal library of books about medical research.

Largely thanks to him, the Treasury was persuaded to agree that a charitable trust could be exempted from tax and estate duty under the 1951 Finance Act. The castle thus became the first major historical property to be recognised by the Treasury for relief from duty under the Act and it meant that the executors had to pay only a little over £500,000 in death duties. In 1974 a fifth codicil was added to Lady Baillie's will, the main purpose of which was to keep the castle as it was and to ensure that her family and also her staff were provided for.

The expectation was that a Foundation would be set up by Lady Baillie, to which the gift could be transferred, but she died before she was able to do that. However, within five weeks of her death everything was in place, including the formation of a charitable company to receive the gift of the castle and an endowment fund of £1.4 million. The company was called Leeds Village Estates Ltd., and Geoffrey Lloyd was one of the trustees.

The company hastily transformed itself into the Leeds Castle Foundation, with trustees chosen from the company trustees, of which Geoffrey Lloyd, who became Lord Geoffrey-Lloyd in 1974, was the first chairman. Everything was transferred to the Foundation at the end of January 1975.

Lady Baillie left about £4.08 million in all, the largest fortune for a woman to be announced in the past twenty years, and much of it was spent on Leeds Castle in one way or another.

Part of the inheritance left to the Foundation was Lady Baillie's two dogs, Great Danes called Boots and Danny, who remained at the castle where they were looked after by Mrs Myra Walsh, the housekeeper, during the week and by Lord Geoffrey-Lloyd at the weekends.

The endowment of £1.4 million was shown to be insufficient for the castle's needs and agreement was reached with the Treasury about the sale of chattels, which realised about £400,000. The London house was sold, as was Harbourside, in the Bahamas, as well as much of the furniture and other items she had collected over the years. Some was bought by her children

At this time, inflation was running at about twenty per cent in this country and Lord Geoffrey-Lloyd decided that the sooner the castle could be opened to the public and making an income, the better. So it was that in 1975 the castle gardens were opened for the first time. Originally, it was intended that there should be a maximum of 15,000 visitors a year, but that proved to be insufficient to create the necessary level of income and in 1976 both house and gardens were opened.

The British-American Tobacco Co agreed to pay £100,000 on top of the conference fee to hold the first conference at Leeds Castle. This persuaded the Trustees that the way ahead was through a fairly aggressive advertising programme. A number of events were organised which were intended both to increase income and to heighten public awareness of the castle.

In May 1977, the castle was chosen as a safe meeting place for European Community ministers attending the seven-nation economic summit. What really turned the spotlight of public attention on Leeds Castle, however, was the Middle East peace conference in July 1978, attended by Foreign Ministers from Israel and Egypt, and the US Secretary of State, Cyrus Vance. Security experts decided the castle was safer than the London hotel that was originally intended as the venue.

Since then, the Foundation has hosted many other events of all kinds, including the annual open-air orchestral concerts. The castle is now Kent's top tourist attraction after Canterbury Cathedral, and is one of the most-visited stately homes in Britain.

Various alterations have had to be made to the grounds, particularly the golf course which was found to be a potential danger to visitors. The Trustees also planted a vineyard on the reputed site of an original vineyard mentioned in the eleventh century Domesday Survey.

Would Lady Baillie have been pleased to know that the home she loved was giving pleasure to so many people? Or did she envisage, in those last months when she was so anxious to settle the castle's future during her lifetime, a quieter, more sedate – perhaps she would have said a more dignified – future for it?

Or perhaps, on the other hand, the last lady of the Ladies' Castle, who lived very much for the moment all her life, would simply have shrugged her elegant shoulders and dismissed the question as irrelevant.

As for Leeds Castle itself, thanks to the care lavished upon it during yet another century, and the promise of continuing care for the future, it can contemplate the new millennium serene in the hope that it will long remain "*the loveliest castle in the world*".

"*the famous and very beautiful seat five miles from Maidstone … with 3,200 acres, of which about one-tenth forms the park.*"

Report of the sale of the castle in *The Times* on 8 February, 1927.

Photo: Angelo Hornak